Bill Tidy's

BOOK of QUOTATIONS

HarperCollins*Publishers*

HarperCollins*Publishers*
P.O. Box, Glasgow G4 ONB

First published 1998

Reprint 10 9 8 7 6 5 4 3 2 1

ISBN 0 00 472179 9

A catalogue record for this book is available from the British Library

Printed and bound in Great Britain by
Caledonian International Book Manufacturing Ltd, Glasgow C64

CONTENTS

FOREWORD

As a veteran of the Accrington Stanley Everest Expedition who has braved the terrors of the Rum 'n' Coco river, escaped from Devil's Island in a doll's pram accompanied by Mad Le Frot, flown with Ludovic Snelgrove the wrestling evangelist, and frequently suffered attacks of docker's paralysis, I am delighted to contribute a foreword to this book. It gives me the chance that all Bill Tidy's admirers long for: to air publicly my enthusiasm for his wonderful Fosdyke Saga, the immortal Cloggies, and such splendid individual cartoons as the Rude Rhymes Detector Van, the Partick Thistle supporter pleading guilty to possession of forged footballs, and the beach attendant advising gentleman paddlers to roll up their trousers because Krakatoa has just erupted.

Nor can I omit the Salford Grey Killer butterfly with its distinctive cough, the Japanese diplomat attempting hara-kiri in Lady Fosdyke's kitchen ("Going to be a long messy job with an egg-whisk, mother"), or the Afghan tribesmen preparing to attack the regimental polo match as soon as a goal is scored, but calling off their assault when the referee disallows it.

This is Bill Tidy's world, a wonderland of comic fantasy which he shares with people like Lewis Carroll, Spike Milligan and Stephen Leacock, for while he is a great cartoonist who in the field of the comic strip is rivalled only by Al Capp and Charles Schultz, it is his mastery of plot and character, his own peculiar lunatic logic, and his insight into the North Country mind that have endeared him and his creations to his devoted followers.

It follows that his Book of Quotations is no ordinary anthology. It reflects the wit and taste and affections of a very funny man and gifted artist, and quite apart from its entertainment value it deserves a place alongside the Oxford and Bartlett and the rest, for there is much here that you will not find elsewhere.

George MacDonald Fraser

INTRODUCTION

Looking back on my selection of quotes I'd hate you to think that for the most part of life on earth, the overwhelming majority of people just stood around, loose-jawed, listening to Groucho Marx and Oscar Wilde one-upping each other.

In truth it's the other way round. Everybody said something! All the deadly duo did was pick up the best bits and gift wrap them. Admittedly a lot of what was said was absolute rubbish but the more I trawled through the sea of quotes the greater treasure of snappy one-, two- or even five-liners were trapped in my net. Many were threadbare with use, others were in evening dress and the odd one or two so new that they are waiting for you to say them in the office or over a plate tomorrow.

Whatever category a quote falls into, it has two great features! In the telling, it's creator can be either acknowledged or it can be passed off as one's own! At this, some may curl their lips in contempt or their moustaches in wax, so make it clear that the art of quotation is remembering the damn things, not who said what to whom! Furthermore, if Groucho and Oscar aren't shouting 'Plagiarist!' and this collection helps and entertains, ignore your critics. They are no more than General Douglas MacArthur of whose carefully arranged pate, Alice Roosevelt Longworth, eldest child of Theodore Roosevelt, said "Never trust a man who combs his hair from his left armpit!"

HE'S HAD IT BRAIDED!

BILL TIDY

Drawing	Speaking	Appearances
Writing	Scripting	Advertising

"Arthur Medlicott does not get ambushed **twice** in the same place!"

Contact website: *http://www.broadband.co.uk/billtidy/*

ACCIDENTS

Coren, Alan **(1938–)** *British humorist, writer and broadcaster*

The Act of God designation on all insurance policies; which means, roughly, that you cannot be insured for the accidents that are most likely to happen to you.

The Lady from Stalingrad Museum (1977), 'A Short History of Insurance'

Graham, Harry **(1874–1936)** *British writer and journalist*

'There's been an accident!' they said,
'Your servant's cut in half; he's dead!'
'Indeed!' said Mr Jones, 'and please
Send me the half that's got my keys.'

Ruthless Rhymes for Heartless Homes (1899), 'Mr Jones'

Grossmith, George and **Weedon** *English humorist writers*

I left the room with silent dignity, but caught my foot in the mat.

Diary of a Nobody (1894)

Punch *British humorous periodical, founded 1841*

What is better than presence of mind in a railway accident? Absence of body. **1849**

Tidy, Bill *Cartoonist*

Caption to cartoon of a man with a polar bear at Titanic Steamship Co. office
But is there any news of the iceberg?

ADVERTISING

Jefferson, Thomas **(1743–1826)** *Third US President*

Advertisements contain the only truths to be relied on in a newspaper.

Letter, 1819

Leacock, Stephen **(1869–1944)** *Canadian humorist and economist*

Advertising may be described as the science of arresting the human intelligence long enough to get money from it.

In Prochow, The Public Speaker's Treasure Chest

Leverhulme, Lord **(1851–1925)** *English soap manufacturer, philanthropist, Liberal politician*

Half the money I spend on advertising is wasted, and the trouble is I don't know which half. **In Ogilvy, Confessions of an Advertising Man (1963)**

Nash, Ogden **(1902–1971)** *American humorous poet*

I think that I shall never see
A billboard lovely as a tree.
Indeed, unless the billboards fall
I'll never see a tree at all. **Happy Days (1933), 'Song of the Open Road'**

Beneath this slab
John Brown is stowed.
He watched the ads,
And not the road. **Good Intentions (1942), 'Lather as You Go'**

ADVICE

Bierce, Ambrose **(1842–c. 1914)** *American writer, journalist and soldier*

Advice: The smallest current coin. **The Cynic's Word Book (1906)**

Harney, Bill **(1895–1962)** *Australian writer of the bush and the Aborigines*

Advice on bush cooking
You always want to garnish it when it's orf.

On long-playing record 'Talkabout', c.1960

Harris, George **(1844–1922)** *American Congregational minister and educator*

In his address to students at the beginning of a new academic year
I intended to give you some advice but now I remember how much is left over from last year unused. **In Braude's Second Encyclopedia (1957)**

Thurber, James **(1894–1961)** *American humorist, writer and illustrator*

Early to rise and early to bed makes a male healthy and wealthy and dead. **The New Yorker, 1939, 'The Shrike and the Chipmunks'**

AGE

Adams, John Quincy **(1767–1848)** *Lawyer and sixth US President*

I inhabit a weak, frail, decayed tenement; battered by the winds and broken in on by the storms, and, from all I can learn, the landlord does not intend to repair. **Attr.**

Adenauer, Konrad **(1876–1967)** *German Christian Democrat Chancellor*

To his doctor
I haven't asked you to make me young again. All I want is to go on getting older. **Attr.**

Allen, Woody **(1935–)** *American film director, writer, actor and comedian*

I recently turned sixty. Practically a third of my life is over.

The Observer Review, 1996

Anonymous

The editors are well under thirty and intend to remain so.

Editorial, The Canadian Mercury, 1928

Ashford, Daisy **(1881–1972)** *English child author*

Mr Salteena was an elderly man of 42 and was fond of asking people to stay with him. **The Young Visiters (1919)**

Astor, Nancy, Viscountess **(1879–1964)** *American-born British Conservative politician; first woman MP*

Refusing to pose for a close-up photograph
Take a close-up of a woman past sixty! You might as well use a picture of a relief map of Ireland! **Attr.**

Auber, Daniel **(1782–1871)** *French opera composer*

Ageing seems to be the only available way to live a long time. **Attr.**

Blake, Eubie **(1883–1983)** *American jazz musician*

He died five days after his hundredth birthday
If I'd known I was gonna live this long, I'd have taken better care of myself. **The Observer, 1983**

Christie, Dame Agatha **(1890–1976)** *English crime novelist and playwright*

DO YOU REMEMBER OUR FIRST CARBON DATE?

An archaeologist is the best husband any woman can have: the older she gets, the more interested he is in her.

News report, 1954; she denied saying it

Cunard, Lady (Maud) 'Emerald' **(1872–1948)**
Granddaughter-in-law of Samuel Cunard, the co-founder of the Cunard Shipping Line

Reply to Somerset Maugham, when said he was leaving early 'to keep his youth'
Then why didn't you bring him with you? I should be delighted to meet him. **In D. Fielding, Emerald and Nancy (1968)**

Grant, Cary **(1904–1986)** *English-born American film actor*

Responding to a telegram received by his agent inquiring: 'How old Cary Grant?'
'Old Cary Grant fine. How you?' **In Halliwell, Filmgoer's Book of Quotes (1973)**

Lehrer, Tom **(1928–)** *American humorist, songwriter and lecturer*

It is sobering to consider that when Mozart was my age he had already been dead for a year. **In N. Shapiro, An Encyclopedia of Quotations about Music**

Marx, Groucho **(1895–1977)** *American film comedian*

A man is only as old as the woman he feels. **Attr.**

I've been around so long, I knew Doris Day before she was a virgin. **Attr.**

Nash, Ogden **(1902–1971)** *American humorous poet*

Do you think my mind is maturing late,
Or simply rotted early? **Good Intentions (1942), 'Lines on Facing Forty'**

Naylor, James Ball **(1860–1945)** *American physician and writer*

King David and King Solomon
Led merry, merry lives,
With many, many lady friends
And many, many wives;
But when old age crept over them,
With many, many qualms,
King Solomon wrote the Proverbs
And King David wrote the Psalms. **'King David and King Solomon' (1935)**

Parkes, Sir Henry **(1815–1896)** *Australian politician, writer and poet*

On being congratulated when he was eighty on the birth of his last child
Don't say my last, you damned fool! Say my latest.
In Randolph Bedford, Naught to Thirty-three

Reagan, Ronald **(1911–)** *Politician and film actor; US President 1981–89*

I am delighted to be with you. In fact, at my age, I am delighted to be anywhere. **Speech at the Oxford Union, 1992**

Smith, Logan Pearsall **(1865–1946)** *American-born British writer*

There is more felicity on the far side of baldness than young men can possibly imagine. **All Trivia (1933), 'Last Words'**

Shaw, George Bernard **(1856–1950)** *Irish dramatist and critic*

On a bust sculpted of him by Rodin

It's a funny thing about that bust. As time goes on it seems to get younger and younger. **In Edwards, More Things I Wish I'd Said**

Wodehouse, P.G. **(1881–1975)** *English novelist*

There is only one cure for grey hair. It was invented by a Frenchman. It is called the guillotine. **The Old Reliable (1951)**

ALCOHOL

Aga Khan III **(1877–1957)** *Muslim leader*

Justifying his liking for alcohol
I'm so holy that when I touch wine, it turns into water.

Attr. in Compton Miller, Who's Really Who (1983)

Benchley, Robert **(1889–1945)** *American humorist and actor*

I must get out of these wet clothes and into a dry martini.

Line delivered in film The Major and the Minor, 1942

Reply when asked if he realised that drinking was a slow death
So who's in a hurry? **Attr.**

Churchill, Randolph **(1911–1968)** *Son of Sir Winston Churchill*

In a letter to a hostess after ruining her dinner party with one of his displays of drunken rudeness
I should never be allowed out in private.

In B. Roberts, Randolph: a Study of Churchill's Son (1984)

Coren, Alan **(1938–)** *British humorist, writer and broadcaster*

Apart from cheese and tulips, the main product of the country [Holland] is advocaat, a drink made from lawyers.

The Sanity Inspector (1974), 'All You Ever Need to Know about Europe'

Lardner, Ring **(1885–1933)** *American humorist, short-story writer and newspaperman*

Speaking to a flamboyantly dressed stranger who walked into the club where he was drinking
How do you look when I'm sober? **In J. Yardley, Ring**

Frenchmen drink wine just like we used to drink water before Prohibition. **In R.E. Drennan, Wit's End**

Nash, Ogden **(1902–1971)** *American humorous poet*

Candy
Is dandy
But liquor
Is quicker. **Hard Lines (1931), 'Reflections on Ice-Breaking'**

Sheridan, Richard Brinsley **(1751–1816)** *Irish comic dramatist*

On being warned that his drinking would destroy the coat of his stomach
Well, then, my stomach must just digest in its waistcoat.

In L. Harris, The Fine Art of Political Wit (1965)

Squire, Sir J.C. **(1884–1958)** *English poet, writer and critic*

But I'm not so think as you drunk I am.

In Baring, One Hundred and One Ballades (1931), 'Ballade of Soporific Absorption'

Thurber, James **(1894–1961)** *American humorist, writer and illustrator*

'Joe,' I said, 'was perhaps the first great nonstop literary drinker of the American nineteenth century. He made the indulgences of Coleridge and De Quincey seem like a bit of mischief in the kitchen with the cooking sherry.'

Alarms and Diversions (1957), 'The Morbundant Life ...'

It's a naïve domestic Burgundy, without any breeding, but I think you'll be amused by its presumption. **Cartoon caption in The New Yorker, 1937**

Whitehorn, Katherine **(1926–)** *English journalist and writer*

The Life and Soul, the man who will never go home while there is one man, woman or glass of anything not yet drunk.

Sunday Best (1976), 'Husband-Swapping'

Wilde, Oscar (1854–1900) *Irish dramatist, novelist, critic and wit*

I have made an important discovery … that alcohol, taken in sufficient quantities, produces all the effects of intoxication. **Attr.**

Wodehouse, P.G. (1881–1975) *English novelist*

It was my Uncle George who discovered that alcohol was a food well in advance of modern medical thought. **The Inimitable Jeeves (1923)**

AMERICA

Anonymous

Overpaid, overfed, oversexed, and over here.

Remark on GIs in Britain during World War II

Fields, W.C. (1880–1946) *American comic film actor*

Last week, I went to Philadelphia, but it was closed. **Attr.**

Harding, Gilbert (1907–1960) *English writer and broadcaster*

Before he [Gilbert Harding] could go to New York he had to get a US visa at the American consulate in Toronto. He was called upon to fill in a long form with many questions, including 'Is it your intention to overthrow the Government of the United States by force?' By the time Harding got to that one he was so irritated that he answered: 'Sole purpose of visit'. **In W. Reyburn, Gilbert Harding (1978)**

Hobson, Sir Harold (1904–1992) *British drama critic and writer*

The United States, I believe, are under the impression that they are twenty years in advance of this country; whilst, as a matter of actual verifiable fact, of course, they are just about six hours behind it.

The Devil in Woodford Wells

Sellar, Walter (1898–1951) and **Yeatman, Robert** (1897–1968) *British humorous writers*

A Bad Thing: America was thus clearly top nation, and History came to a . **1066 And All That (1930)**

Toynbee, Arnold **(1889–1975)** *English historian and scholar*

America is a large, friendly dog in a very small room. Every time it wags its tail it knocks over a chair. **Broadcast news summary, 1954**

ANGER AND DISAPPROVAL

Diller, Phyllis **(1917–1974)** *American comedian*

Never go to bed mad. Stay up and fight. **Phyllis Diller's Housekeeping Hints**

Wodehouse, P.G. **(1881–1975)** *English novelist*

He spoke with a certain what-is-it in his voice, and I could see that, if not actually disgruntled, he was far from being gruntled.

The Code of the Woosters (1938)

Ice formed on the butler's upper slopes. **Pigs Have Wings (1952)**

ANIMALS

Barbellion, W.N.P. **(1889–1919)** *English diarist and naturalist*

Am writing an essay on the life-history of insects and have abandoned the idea of writing on 'How Cats Spend their Time'.

The Journal of a Disappointed Man (1919)

Belloc, Hilaire **(1870–1953)** *French-born English writer and poet*

I shoot the Hippopotamus
with bullets made of platinum,
Because if I use leaden ones
his hide is sure to flatten 'em.

The Bad Child's Book of Beasts (1896), 'The Hippopotamus'

Mothers of large families (who claim to common sense)
Will find a Tiger well repays the trouble and expense.

The Bad Child's Book of Beasts (1896), 'The Tiger'

I had an Aunt in Yucatan
Who bought a Python from a man
And kept it for a pet.
She died, because she never knew
These simple little rules and few –
The Snake is living yet. **More Beasts for Worse Children (1897), 'The Python'**

Bennett, Alan **(1934–)** *English dramatist, actor and diarist*

On dogs

It's the one species I wouldn't mind seeing vanish from the face of the earth. I wish they were like the white rhino – six of them left in the Serengeti National Park, and all males. **Attr.**

Carroll, Lewis **(1832–1898)** *English mathematician and children's novelist*

He thought he saw a Buffalo
Upon the chimney-piece:
He looked again, and found it was
His sister's husband's niece.
'Unless you leave this house,' he said,
'I'll send for the Police!'
He thought he saw a Rattlesnake
That questioned him in Greek,
He looked again and found it was
The Middle of Next Week.
'The one thing I regret,' he said,
'Is that it cannot speak!' **Sylvie and Bruno (1889)**

He thought he saw a Banker's Clerk
Descending from the bus:
He looked again, and found it was
A Hippopotamus:
'If this should stay to dine,' he said,
'There won't be much for us.' **Sylvie and Bruno (1889)**

Congreve, William **(1670–1729)** *English dramatist and poet*

I confess freely to you, I could never look long upon a monkey, without very mortifying reflections.

Letter to Mr Dennis, concerning Humour in Comedy, 1695

Coward, Sir Noël **(1899–1973)** *English dramatist, actor and composer*

Reply to Laurence Olivier's five-year-old daughter, Tamsin, when she asked what two dogs were doing together

The doggie in front has suddenly gone blind, and the other one has very kindly offered to push him all the way to St Dunstan's.

In K. Tynan, The Sound of Two Hands Clapping (1975)

Cuppy, Will **(1884–1949)** *American humorist and critic*

The Dodo never had a chance. He seems to have been invented for the sole purpose of becoming extinct and that was all he was good for.

How to Become Extinct (1941)

Dressler, Marie **(1869–1934)** *American comic film actress*

If ants are such busy workers, how come they find time to go to all the picnics? **In Cowan, The Wit of Women**

Merritt, Dixon Lanier **(1879–1972)** *American editor*

A wonderful bird is the pelican,
His bill will hold more than his belican.
He can take in his beak
Food enough for a week,
But I'm damned if I see how the helican. **Nashville Banner, 1913**

Muir, Frank **(1920–1998)** *English writer, humorist and broadcaster*

Dogs, like horses, are quadrupeds. That is to say, they have four rupeds, one at each corner, on which they walk.

You Can't Have Your Kayak and Heat It, with Dennis Norden

Nash, Ogden **(1902–1971)** *American humorous poet*

The turtle lives 'twixt plated decks
Which practically conceal its sex.
I think it clever of the turtle
In such a fix to be so fertile. **Hard Lines (1931), 'The Turtle'**

The cow is of the bovine ilk;
One end is moo, the other, milk. **Free Wheeling (1931), 'The Cow'**

The song of canaries
Never varies,
And when they're moulting
They're pretty revolting. **The Face is Familiar (1940), 'The Canary'**

A door is what a dog is perpetually on the wrong side of.

The Private Dining Room (1952), 'A Dog's Best Friend Is His Illiteracy'

Parker, Dorothy **(1893–1967)** *American poet, writer, critic and wit*

It costs me never a stab nor squirm
To tread by chance upon a worm.
'Aha, my little dear,' I say,
'Your clan will pay me back one day.'

Sunset Gun, 'Thoughts for a Sunshiny Morning'

Peacock, Thomas Love **(1785–1866)** *English novelist and poet*

The mountain sheep are sweeter,
But the valley sheep are fatter;
We therefore deemed it meeter
To carry off the latter.

The Misfortunes of Elphin (1823), 'The War-Song of Dinas Vawr'

Punch *British humorous periodical, founded 1841*

Cats is 'dogs' and rabbits is 'dogs' and so's Parrats, but this 'ere 'Tortis' is an insect, and there ain't no charge for it. **1869**

There was one poor tiger that hadn't got a Christian. **1875**

Saki (Hector Hugh Munro) **(1870–1916)** *British journalist and writer*

In baiting a mouse-trap with cheese, always leave room for the mouse.

The Square Egg (1924), 'The Infernal Parliament'

Sheridan, Richard Brinsley **(1751–1816)** *Irish comic dramatist*

She's as headstrong as an allegory on the banks of the Nile.

The Rivals (1775)

Wilberforce, Bishop Samuel **(1805–1873)** *English prelate*

If I were a cassowary
On the plains of Timbuctoo,
I would eat a missionary,
Cassock, band, and hymn-book too.

Attr. impromptu verse; also attributed to W.M. Thackeray

Yeatman, Robert **(1897–1968)** *British humorous writer*

To confess that you are totally Ignorant about the Horse, is social suicide: you will be despised by everybody, especially the horse.

Horse Nonsense (1933); with W.C. Sellar

APPEARANCE

Amis, Kingsley **(1922–1995)** *English writer, poet and critic*

Outside every fat man there was an even fatter man trying to close in.

One Fat Englishman (1963)

Beerbohm, Sir Max **(1872–1956)** *English writer and caricaturist*

Great men are but life-sized. Most of them, indeed, are rather short. **Attr.**

Chesterton, G.K. **(1874–1936)** *English novelist, poet and critic*

On being stuck in the door of a car, he said it reminded him of the words of an old Irishman
'Why don't you get out sideways?'
'I have no sideways.' **In M. Ward, Gilbert Keith Chesterton (1944)**

Suggesting that being fat has its compensations
Just the other day in the Underground I enjoyed the pleasure of offering my seat to three ladies.

In W. Scholz, Das Buch des Lachens

Marx, Groucho **(1895–1977)** *American film comedian*

There's a man outside with a big black moustache.
– Tell him I've got one. **Horse Feathers, film, 1932**

Parton, Dolly **(1946–)** *American country singer and songwriter*

You'd be surprised how much it costs to look this cheap.

In Carole McKenzie, Quotable Women (1992)

Richards, Sir Gordon **(1904–1986)** *British champion jockey and trainer*

Referring to his height, when he learned of his knighthood
Mother always told me my day was coming, but I never realized I'd end up being the shortest knight of the year. **Attr.**

Wodehouse, P.G. **(1881–1975)** *English novelist*

Her hair was a deep chestnut, her eyes blue, her nose small and laid back with about as much loft as a light iron.

The Heart of a Goof (1926), 'Chester Forgets Himself'

ARCHITECTURE

Carroll, Lewis (1832–1898) *English mathematician and children's novelist*

After seeing the new Gilbert Scott belfry at Christ Church, Oxford
The advantage of having been born in the reign of Queen Anne, and of having died in that or the subsequent reign, has never been so painfully apparent as it is now. **The Works of Lewis Carroll (1965)**

Lette, Kathy (1958–) *Australian author*

Inner-city council estates make you believe the world was really built in six days. **Mad Cows (1996)**

Wright, Frank Lloyd (1869–1959) *American architect and writer*

The physician can bury his mistakes, but the architect can only advise his client to plant vines. **New York Times Magazine, 1953**

THE ARMED FORCES

Churchill, Sir Winston (1874–1965) *English statesman*

Don't talk to me about naval tradition. It's nothing but rum, sodomy and the lash. **In Gretton, Former Naval Person (1968)**

Heller, Joseph (1923–) *American novelist*

I had examined myself pretty thoroughly and discovered that I was unfit for military service. **Catch-22 (1961)**

Milligan, Spike (1918–) *English humorist*

The Army works like this: if a man dies when you hang him, keep hanging him until he gets used to it. **Attr.**

Sellar, Walter (1898–1951) and **Yeatman, Robert** (1897–1968)
British humorous writers

Napoleon's armies always used to march on their stomachs, shouting: 'Vive l'Intérieur!' and so moved about very slowly.

1066 And All That (1930)

Truman, Harry S. **(1884–1972)** *US President 1945–53*

Of General MacArthur

I didn't fire him because he was a dumb son of a bitch, although he was, but that's not against the law for generals. If it was, half to three-quarters of them would be in gaol. **In Merle Miller, Plain Speaking (1974)**

Voltaire **(1694–1778)** *French author and critic*

Referring to the execution of the English Admiral Byng for refusing to attack a French fleet

Dans ce pays-ci il est bon de tuer de temps en temps un amiral pour encourager les autres. [In this country it is considered a good idea to kill an admiral from time to time, to encourage the others.]

Candide (1759)

Wellington, Arthur Wellesley, Duke of **(1769–1852)**
Irish soldier and statesman

I don't know what effect these men will have upon the enemy, but, by God, they frighten me. **Attr.**

ART AND ARTISTS

Beaverbrook, Lord **(1879–1964)** *British newspaper proprietor and politician*

Buy old masters. They fetch a better price than old mistresses. **Attr.**

Chesterton, G.K. **(1874–1936)** *English novelist, poet and critic*

The artistic temperament is a disease that afflicts amateurs.

Heretics (1905)

Herbert, Sir A.P. **(1890–1971)** *English writer and politician*

As my poor father used to say
In 1863,
Once people start on all this Art
Good-bye, moralitee!
And what my father used to say
Is good enough for me.

Ballads for Broadbrows (1930), 'Lines for a Worthy Person'

A highbrow is the kind of person who looks at a sausage and thinks of Picasso. **Attr.**

Hughes, Billy (1862–1952) *Australian statesman and Prime Minister, 1915–23*

To his portrait painter
My man, I don't want justice, I want mercy.

In David Low, Low's Autobiography

Punch *British humorous periodical, founded 1841*

Botticelli isn't a wine, you Juggins! Botticelli's a cheese! **1894**

Rogers, Will (1879–1935) *American comic actor, rancher, writer and wit*

Message to his niece on a postcard of the Venus de Milo
See what will happen to you if you don't stop biting your fingernails. **Attr.**

Sargent, John Singer (1856–1925) *American painter*

Every time I paint a portrait I lose a friend.

In N. Bentley and E. Esar, Treasury of Humorous Quotations (1951)

Shahn, Ben **(1898–1969)** *American painter and muralist, born in Lithuania*

Outlining the difference between professional and amateur painters
An amateur is an artist who supports himself with outside jobs which enable him to paint. A professional is someone whose wife works to enable him to paint. **Attr.**

Thurber, James **(1894–1961)** *American humorist, writer and illustrator*

He knows all about art, but he doesn't know what he likes.
Cartoon caption

You wait here and I'll bring the etchings down. **Cartoon caption**

Ustinov, Sir Peter **(1921–)** *English actor, dramatist, writer and wit*

If Botticelli were alive today he'd be working for Vogue.
The Observer, 'Sayings of the Week', 1962

Wharton, Edith **(1862–1937)** *American writer*

Mrs Ballinger is one of the ladies who pursue Culture in bands, as though it were dangerous to meet it alone.
Xingu and Other Stories (1916), Title story

Whistler, James McNeill **(1834–1903)** *American painter and etcher*

To a lady who said the two greatest painters were himself and Velasquez
'Why,' answered Whistler in dulcet tones, 'why drag in Velasquez?'
In D.C. Seitz, Whistler Stories (1913)

Replying to a sitter's complaint that his portrait was not a great work of art
Perhaps not, but then you can't call yourself a great work of nature.
In D.C. Seitz, Whistler Stories (1913)

Wilde, Oscar **(1854–1900)** *Irish dramatist, novelist, critic and wit*

On the artist James Whistler
With our James vulgarity begins at home, and should be allowed to stay there. **Letter to the World**

ATHEISM

Buchan, John **(1875–1940)** *Scottish writer and statesman*

An atheist is a man who has no invisible means of support. **Attr.**

Buñuel, Luis (1900–1983) *Spanish surrealist film director*

I am still an atheist, thank God. **Attr.**

BEAUTY

Saki (Hector Hugh Munro) (1870–1916) *British journalist and writer*

I always say beauty is only sin deep.

Reginald (1904), 'Reginald's Choir Treat'

Marx, Groucho (1895–1977) *American film comedian*

You're the most beautiful woman I've ever seen, which doesn't say much for you. **Animal Crackers, film, 1930**

BIOGRAPHY

Arbuthnot, John (1667–1735) *Scottish physician, pamphleteer and wit*

Of biography

One of the new terrors of death. **In Carruthers, Life of Pope (1857)**

Bentley, Edmund Clerihew **(1875–1956)** *English journalist*

The art of Biography
Is different from Geography.
Geography is about Maps,
But Biography is about chaps.

Chapman and Hall
Swore not at all.
Mr Chapman's yea was yea,
And Mr Hall's nay was nay.

What I like about Clive
Is that he is no longer alive.
There is a great deal to be said
For being dead.

Sir Humphrey Davy
Abominated gravy.
He lived in the odium
Of having discovered Sodium.

Edward the Confessor
Slept under the dresser.
When that began to pall
He slept in the hall.

John Stuart Mill,
By a mighty effort of will,
Overcame his natural bonhomie
And wrote 'Principles of Political Economy'.

Sir Christopher Wren
Said, 'I am going to dine with some men.
If anybody calls
Say I am designing St Paul's.' **Biography for Beginners (1905)**

George the Third
Ought never to have occurred.
One can only wonder
At so grotesque a blunder. **More Biography (1929)**

When their lordships asked Bacon
How many bribes he had taken
He had at least the grace
To get very red in the face. **Baseless Biography (1939)**

Thurber, James (1894–1961) *American humorist, writer and illustrator*

I suppose that the high-water mark of my youth in Columbus, Ohio, was the night the bed fell on my father. **My Life and Hard Times (1933)**

BOOKS

Belloc, Hilaire (1870–1953) *French-born English writer and poet*

When I am dead, I hope it may be said:
'His sins were scarlet, but his books were read.' **Sonnets and Verse (1923)**

Borges, Jorge Luis (1899–1986) *Argentinian writer, poet and librarian*

On Henley's translation of Beckford's Vathek

El original es infiel a la traducción. [The original is not faithful to the translation.] **Sobre el 'Vathek' de William Beckford (1943)**

Disraeli, Benjamin (1804–1881) *English statesman and novelist*

His customary reply to those who sent him unsolicited manuscripts

Thank you for the manuscript; I shall lose no time in reading it. **Attr.**

Evans, Dame Edith (1888–1976) *English stage and film actress*

On being told that Nancy Mitford had been lent a villa to enable her to finish a book

Oh really. What exactly is she reading? **Attr.**

Goldsmith, Oliver (1728–1774) *Irish novelist, playwright and poet*

A book may be amusing with numerous errors, or it may be very dull without a single absurdity. **The Vicar of Wakefield (1766)**

James, Brian (1892–1972) *Australian writer*

The book of my enemy has been remaindered
And I am pleased. **'The Book of My Enemy Has Been Remaindered'**

Lichtenberg, Georg **(1742–1799)** *German writer*

There can hardly be a stranger commodity in the world than books. Printed by people who don't understand them; sold by people who don't understand them; bound, criticized and read by people who don't understand them, and now even written by people who don't understand them. **A Doctrine of Scattered Occasions**

Macaulay, Dame Rose **(1881–1958)** *English novelist and travel writer*

It was a book to kill time for those who like it better dead. **Attr.**

Orton, Joe **(1933–1967)** *English dramatist*

Reading isn't an occupation we encourage among police officers. We try to keep the paper work down to a minimum. **Loot (1967)**

Reed, Henry **(1914–1986)** *English poet*

I have known her pass the whole evening without mentioning a single book, or in fact anything unpleasant, at all. **A Very Great Man Indeed (1953)**

Smith, Logan Pearsall **(1865–1946)** *American-born British writer*

A best-seller is the gilded tomb of a mediocre talent. **Afterthoughts (1931)**

Waugh, Evelyn **(1903–1966)** *English journalist and novelist*

Particularly against books the Home Secretary is. If we can't stamp out literature in the country, we can at least stop it being brought in from outside. **Vile Bodies (1930)**

Wilde, Oscar **(1854–1900)** *Irish dramatist, novelist, critic and wit*

I never travel without my diary. One should always have something sensational to read in the train. **The Importance of Being Earnest (1895)**

In a lecture on Dickens
One would have to have a heart of stone to read the death of Little Nell without laughing. **In H. Pearson, Lives of the Wits**

BOREDOM

Bierce, Ambrose **(1842–c. 1914)** *American writer, journalist and soldier*

Bore: A person who talks when you wish him to listen.
The Cynic's Word Book (1906)

Freud, Clement (1924–) *British politician, broadcaster and writer*

If you resolve to give up smoking, drinking and loving, you don't actually live longer; it just seems longer. **The Observer, 1964**

Howells, W.D. (1837–1920) *American novelist and literary critic*

Some people can stay longer in an hour than others can in a week.

In Esar (ed.), Treasury of Humorous Quotations (1951)

Mencken, H.L. (1880–1956) *American journalist and linguist*

The chief contribution of Protestantism to human thought is its massive proof that God is a bore. **Notebooks (1956), 'Minority Report'**

Saki (Hector Hugh Munro) (1870–1916) *British journalist and writer*

'I believe I take precedence,' he said coldly; 'you are merely the club Bore; I am the club Liar.'

Beasts and Super-Beasts (1914), 'A Defensive Diamond'

Steele, Sir Richard **(1672–1729)** *Irish-born English writer and politician*

It is to be noted, That when any Part of this Paper appears dull, there is a Design in it. **The Tatler, 1709**

Taylor, Bert Leston **(1866–1921)** *American columnist*

A bore is a man who, when you ask him how he is, tells you.

The So-Called Human Race (1922)

Thomas, Dylan **(1914–1953)** *Welsh poet*

Dylan talked copiously, then stopped.
'Somebody's boring me,' he said, 'I think it's me.'

In Heppenstall, Four Absentees (1960)

Updike, John **(1932–)** *American novelist, short-story writer, poet and critic*

A healthy male adult bore consumes one and a half times his own weight in other people's patience.

Assorted Prose (1965), 'Confessions of a Wild Bore'

BUREAUCRACY

Anonymous

Notice in a Government office, London
Due to financial restraints, the light at the end of the tunnel has been switched off until further notice. **The Herald, 1996**

Anonymous

A committee is a cul-de-sac down which ideas are lured and then quietly strangled. **New Scientist, 1973**

A camel is a horse designed by a committee.

This is a rotten argument, but it should be good enough for their lordships on a hot summer afternoon. **Annotation in ministerial brief**

Huxley, Aldous **(1894–1963)** *English novelist*

Official dignity tends to increase in inverse ratio to the importance of the country in which the office is held. **Beyond the Mexique Bay (1934)**

Sampson, Anthony (1926–) *British writer and journalist*

Of the Civil Service

Members rise from CMG (known sometimes in Whitehall as 'Call Me God') to the KCMG ('Kindly Call Me God') to ... the GCMG ('God Calls Me God'). **The Anatomy of Britain (1962)**

Samuel, Lord (1870–1963) *English statesman, philosopher and administrator*

Referring to the Civil Service

A difficulty for every solution. **Attr.**

BUSINESS

Anonymous

A Company for carrying on an undertaking of Great Advantage, but no one to know what it is. **The South Sea Company Prospectus**

Our company absorbs the cost.

Useful Arab phrase in modern Arab-English phrase book for American oil engineers

Barnum, Phineas T. (1810–1891) *American showman*

Every crowd has a silver lining. **Attr.**

Betjeman, Sir John (1906–1984) *English poet*

You ask me what it is I do. Well actually, you know,
I'm partly a liaison man and partly P.R.O.
Essentially I integrate the current export drive
And basically I'm viable from ten o'clock till five. **'Executive' (1974)**

Galbraith, J.K. (1908–) *Canadian-born American economist and author*

The salary of the chief executive of the large corporation is not a market award for achievement. It is frequently in the nature of a warm personal gesture by the individual to himself. **Annals of an Abiding Liberal (1980)**

Murdoch, Rupert (1931–) *Media tycoon*

Monopoly is a terrible thing, till you have it. **The New Yorker, 1979**

Wilson, Charles E. (1890–1961) *American politician*

What is good for the country is good for General Motors, and vice versa. **Remark to Congressional Committee, 1953**

CAUTION

Belloc, Hilaire (1870–1953) *French-born English writer and poet*

And always keep a-hold of Nurse
For fear of finding something worse. **Cautionary Tales (1907), 'Jim'**

Twain, Mark **(1835–1910)** *American humorist and novelist*

It is by the goodness of God that in our country we have those three unspeakably precious things: freedom of speech, freedom of conscience, and the prudence never to practise either of them.

Following the Equator (1897)

CERTAINTY

Goldwyn, Samuel **(1882–1974)** *Polish-born American film producer*

I'll give you a definite maybe. **In Colombo, Wit and Wisdom of the Moviemakers**

Guedalla, Philip **(1889–1944)** *English historian, biographer and lawyer*

People who jump to conclusions rarely alight on them.

The Observer, 'Sayings of the Week', 1924

CHILDREN

Amis, Kingsley **(1922–1995)** *English writer, poet and critic*

It was no wonder that people were so horrible when they started life as children. **One Fat Englishman (1963)**

Hilaire **(1870–1953)** *French-born English writer and poet*

The chief defect of Henry King,
Was chewing little bits of String ...

Physicians of the Utmost Fame
Were called at once; but when they came
They answered, as they took their Fees,
'There is no Cure for this Disease.' ...

'Oh, my Friends, be warned by me,
That Breakfast, Dinner, Lunch, and Tea
Are all the Human Frame requires ...'
With that, the Wretched Child expires. **Cautionary Tales (1907), 'Henry King'**

Carroll, Lewis (1832–1898) *English mathematician and children's novelist*

I am fond of children (except boys). **Letter to Kathleen Eschwege, 1879**

Inge, William Ralph (1860–1954) *English prelate and mathematician*

The proper time to influence the character of a child is about a hundred years before he is born. **The Observer, 1929**

Knox, Ronald (1888–1957) *English Roman Catholic priest and theologian*

Definition of a baby

A loud noise at one end and no sense of responsibility at the other. **Attr.**

Marryat, Frederick (1792–1848) *English naval officer and novelist*

Of an illegitimate baby

If you please, ma'am, it was a very little one. **Mr Midshipman Easy (1836)**

Marx, Groucho (1895–1977) *American film comedian*

Why, a four-year old could understand this report. Run out and find me a four-year old child. **Duck Soup, film, 1933**

Nash, Ogden (1902–1971) *American humorous poet*

A bit of talcum
Is always walcum. **Free Wheeling (1931), 'Reflection on Babies'**

Children aren't happy with nothing to ignore,
And that's what parents were created for. **Happy Days (1933), 'The Parent'**

Vidal, Gore (1925–) *American novelist, dramatist, essayist, critic and poet*

Never have children, only grandchildren. **Two Sisters (1970)**

CHRISTIANITY

Allen, Dave (1936–) *Irish comedian and TV personality*

Referring to the nuns who educated him

The Gestapo in drag. **Attr.**

Allen, Woody (1935–) *American film director, writer, actor and comedian*

The lion and the calf shall lie down together but the calf won't get much sleep. **Without Feathers (1976)**

Ashford, Daisy **(1881–1972)** *English child author*

Bernard always had a few prayers in the hall and some whiskey afterwards as he was rarther pious but Mr Salteena was not very addicted to prayers so he marched up to bed.

The Young Visiters (1919)

Belloc, Hilaire **(1870–1953)** *French-born English writer and poet*

I always like to associate with a lot of priests because it makes me understand anti-clerical things so well. **Attr.**

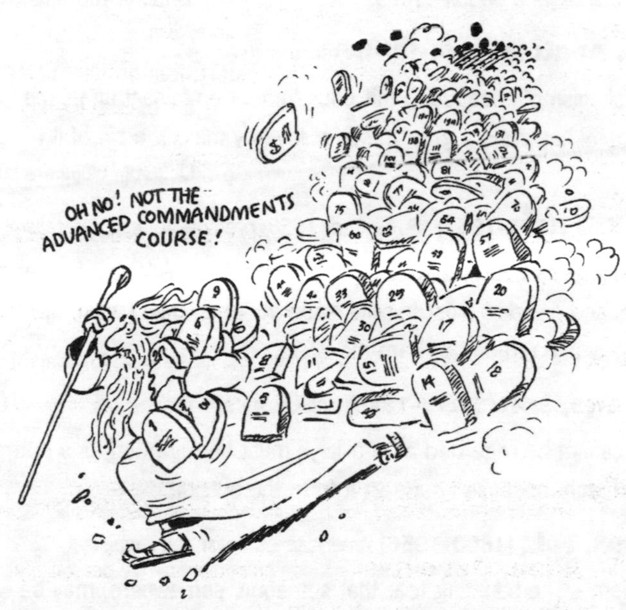

Suggested rider to the Ten Commandments

Candidates should not attempt more than six of these. **Attr.**

Bruce, Lenny **(1925–1966)** *American comedian, prosecuted for obscenity*

Referring to the Crucifixion

It was just one of those parties which got out of hand.

The Guardian, 1979

Chaplin, Charlie **(1889–1977)** *English comedian, film actor, director and satirist*

Priest: May the Lord have mercy on your soul.

Verdoux: Why not? After all, it belongs to Him. **Monsieur Verdoux (1947)**

Dix, George **(1901–1952)** *English Anglican Benedictine monk, historian and liturgical scholar*

It is no accident that the symbol of a bishop is a crook, and the sign of an archbishop is a double-cross. **Letter to The Times, 1977**

France, Anatole **(1844–1924)** *French writer*

Le Christianisme a beaucoup fait pour l'amour en faisant un péché.

[Christianity has done a great deal for love by making a sin of it.]

Le Jardin d'Epicure (1894)

John XXIII **(1881–1963)** *Pope from 1958; promoter of ecumenicalism*

It often happens that I wake at night and begin to think about a serious problem and decide I must tell the Pope about it. Then I wake up completely and remember I am the Pope. **Attr.**

Melbourne, Lord **(1779–1848)** *English statesman*

While I cannot be regarded as a pillar, I must be regarded as a buttress of the church, because I support it from the outside. **Attr.**

Mencken, H.L. **(1880–1956)** *American journalist and linguist*

Puritanism – The haunting fear that someone, somewhere, may be happy. **A Mencken Chrestomathy (1949)**

Russell, Bertrand **(1872–1970)** *Welsh philosopher, mathematician and author*

There's a Bible on that shelf there. But I keep it next to Voltaire – poison and antidote. **In Harris, Kenneth Harris Talking To: (1971)**

Saki (Hector Hugh Munro) (1870–1916) *British journalist and writer*

People may say what they like about the decay of Christianity; the religious system that produced green Chartreuse can never really die.

Reginald (1904), 'Reginald on Christmas Presents'

Tucholsky, Kurt (1890–1935) *German satirist and writer*

Was die Kirche nicht verhindern kann, das segnet sie. [What the church can't prevent, it blesses.] **Schnipsel (Scraps, 1973)**

Twain, Mark (1835–1910) *American humorist and novelist*

Most people are bothered by those passages in Scripture which they cannot understand; but as for me, I always noticed that the passages in Scripture which trouble me most are those that I do understand.

In Simcox, Treasury of Quotations on Christian Themes

Wellington, Arthur Wellesley, Duke of (1769–1852)
Irish soldier and statesman

Responding to a vicar's enquiry as to whether there was anything he would like his forthcoming sermon to be about
Yes, about ten minutes. **Attr.**

Ybarra, Thomas Russell (b. 1880) *American journalist and poet*

A Christian is a man who feels
Repentance on a Sunday
For what he did on Saturday
And is going to do on Monday. **'The Christian' (1909)**

CIVILIZATION

Gandhi (1869–1948) *Indian political leader*

When asked what he thought of Western civilization
I think it would be an excellent idea. **Attr.**

Garrod, Heathcote William (1878–1960) *English classical scholar*

In response to criticism that, during World War I, he was not fighting to defend civilization
Madam, I am the civilization they are fighting to defend.

In D. Balsdon, Oxford Now and Then (1970)

Knox, Ronald **(1888–1957)** *English Roman Catholic priest and theologian*

It is so stupid of modern civilization to have given up believing in the devil when he is the only explanation of it. **Attr.**

Paglia, Camille **(1947–)** *American author and critic*

If civilization had been left in female hands, we would still be living in grass huts. **Sex, Art and American Culture: Essays (1992)**

Park, Mungo **(1771–1806)** *Scottish explorer*

Remark on finding a gibbet in an unexplored part of Africa
The sight of it gave me infinite pleasure, as it proved that I was in a civilized society. **Attr.**

Ashford, Daisy **(1881–1972)** *English child author*

My dear Clincham, The bearer of this letter is an old friend of mine not quite the right side of the blanket as they say in fact he is the son of a first rate butcher but his mother was a decent family called Hyssopps of the Glen so you see he is not so bad and is desireus of being the correct article. **The Young Visiters (1919)**

Belloc, Hilaire **(1870–1953)** *French-born English writer and poet*

Like many of the Upper Class
He liked the Sound of Broken Glass.

New Cautionary Tales (1930), 'About John who Lost a Fortune Throwing Stones'

Bossidy, John Collins **(1860–1928)** *American oculist*

And this is good old Boston,
The home of the bean and the cod,
Where the Lowells talk only to Cabots,
And the Cabots talk only to God. **Toast at Harvard dinner, 1910**

Brough, Robert Barnabas **(1828–1860)** *English writer*

My Lord Tomnoddy is thirty-four;
The Earl can last but a few years more.
My Lord in the Peers will take his place:
Her Majesty's councils his words will grace.

Office he'll hold and patronage sway;
Fortunes and lives he will vote away;
And what are his qualifications? – ONE!
He's the Earl of Fitzdotterel's eldest son. **'My Lord Tomnoddy' (1855)**

Cartland, Barbara **(1902–)** *English romantic novelist*

When asked in a radio interview whether she thought that British class barriers had broken down

Of course they have, or I wouldn't be sitting here talking to someone like you. **In J. Cooper, Class (1979)**

Curzon, Lord **(1859–1925)** *English statesman*

On seeing some soldiers bathing

I never knew the lower classes had such white skins. **Attr.**

Sitwell, Dame Edith **(1887–1964)** *English poet, critic and biographer*

A pompous woman of his acquaintance, complaining that the head-waiter of a restaurant had not shown her and her husband immediately to a table, said: 'We had to tell him who we were.' Gerald, interested, enquired, 'And who were you?' **Taken Care Of (1965)**

Theroux, Paul **(1941–)** *American novelist and travel writer*

The ship follows Soviet custom: it is riddled with class distinctions so subtle, it takes a trained Marxist to appreciate them.

The Great Railway Bazaar (1975)

Thiers, Louis Adolphe **(1797–1877)** *French statesman and historian*

Defending his social status after someone had remarked that his mother had been a cook

She was – but I assure you that she was a very bad cook. **Attr.**

West, Dame Rebecca **(1892–1983)** *English novelist, journalist and critic*

Cable sent to Noël Coward after learning they had both been on a Nazi death list

My dear – the people we should have been seen dead with.

Times Literary Supplement, 1982

Wodehouse, P.G. **(1881–1975)** *English novelist*

Unlike the male codfish which, suddenly finding itself the parent of three million five hundred thousand little codfish, cheerfully resolves to love them all, the British aristocracy is apt to look with a somewhat jaundiced eye on its younger sons. **In R. Usborne, Wodehouse at Work to the End (1976), 5**

COMMUNISM

Anonymous

Capitalism is the exploitation of man by man. Communism is the complete opposite. **Described by Laurence J. Peter as a 'Polish proverb'**

Elliott, Ebenezer (1781–1849) *English poet and merchant*

What is a communist? One who hath yearnings
For equal division of unequal earnings. **Epigram, 1850**

Morley, Robert (1908–1992) *British stage and film actor*

There's no such thing in Communist countries as a load of old cod's wallop, the cod's wallop is always fresh made. **Punch, 1974**

Smith, F.E. (1872–1930) *English lawyer and statesman*

On Bolshevism
Nature has no cure for this sort of madness, though I have known a legacy from a rich relative work wonders. **Law, Life and Letters (1927)**

COMPASSION

Graham, Harry (1874–1936) *British writer and journalist*

Billy, in one of his nice new sashes,
Fell in the fire and was burnt to ashes;
Now, although the room grows chilly,
I haven't the heart to poke poor Billy.

Ruthless Rhymes for Heartless Homes (1899), 'Tender-Heartedness'

Huxley, Aldous (1894–1963) *English novelist*

She was a machine-gun riddling her hostess with sympathy.

Mortal Coils (1922)

Wilde, Oscar (1854–1900) *Irish dramatist, novelist, critic and wit*

Anybody can sympathise with the sufferings of a friend, but it requires a very fine nature to sympathise with a friend's success.

'The Soul of Man under Socialism' (1881)

CONSCIENCE

Mencken, H.L. **(1880–1956)** *American journalist and linguist*

Conscience is the inner voice that warns us somebody may be looking.

A Mencken Chrestomathy (1949)

Nash, Ogden **(1902–1971)** *American humorous poet*

He who is ridden by a conscience
Worries about a lot of nonscience;
He without benefit of scruples
His fun and income soon quadruples.

The Face is Familiar (1940), 'Reflection on the Fallibility of Nemesis'

CONTEMPT

Ashford, Daisy **(1881–1972)** *English child author*

Ethel patted her hair and looked very sneery. **The Young Visiters (1919)**

Bierce, Ambrose **(1842–c. 1914)** *American writer, journalist and soldier*

Contempt: The feeling of a prudent man for an enemy who is too formidable safely to be opposed. **The Enlarged Devil's Dictionary (1961)**

COWARDICE

Carroll, Lewis **(1832–1898)** *English mathematician and children's novelist*

'I'm very brave generally,' he went on in a low voice: 'only to-day I happen to have a headache.' **Through the Looking-Glass (1872)**

Johnston, Brian **(1912–1994)** *Broadcaster and cricket commentator*

When asked by his commanding officer what steps he would take if he came across a German battalion

Long ones, backwards. **Quoted in his obituary, Sunday Times**

Sheridan, Richard Brinsley **(1751–1816)** *Irish comic dramatist*

My valour is certainly going! – it is sneaking off! – I feel it oozing out as it were at the palms of my hands! **The Rivals (1775)**

Ustinov, Sir Peter (1921–) *English actor, dramatist, writer and wit*

Courage is often lack of insight, whereas cowardice in many cases is based on good information. **Attr.**

Voltaire (1694–1778) *French author and critic*

Marriage is the only adventure open to the cowardly. **Attr.**

CRIME

Allen, Fred (1894–1956) *American comedian*

He's a good boy; everything he steals he brings right home to his mother. **Attr.**

Balzac, Honoré de (1799–1850) *French novelist*

Remark made on waking to find a burglar in his room
I am laughing to think what risks you take to try to find money in a desk by night where the legal owner can never find any by day. **Attr.**

De Quincey, Thomas (1785–1859) *English writer and critic*

If a man once indulges himself in murder, very soon he comes to think little of robbing; and from robbing he comes next to drinking and sabbath-breaking, and from that to incivility and procrastination.
'Murder Considered as One of the Fine Arts' (1839)

Henry, O. (1862–1910) *American writer*

A burglar who respects his art always takes his time before taking anything else. **Makes the Whole World Kin**

CRITICISM

Behan, Brendan (1923–1964) *Irish author*

Critics are like eunuchs in a harem: they know how it's done, they've seen it done every day, but they're unable to do it themselves. **Attr.**

Conran, Shirley (1932–) *English author*

On Julie Burchill
I cannot take seriously the criticism of someone who doesn't know how to use a semicolon. **Attr.**

Hampton, Christopher **(1946–)** *English dramatist*

Asking a working writer what he thinks about critics is like asking a lamp-post how it feels about dogs. **The Sunday Times Magazine, 1977**

Liberace **(1919–1987)** *American pianist*

Remark made after hostile criticism
I cried all the way to the bank. **Autobiography (1973)**

Marx, Groucho **(1895–1977)** *American film comedian*

I was so long writing my review that I never got around to reading the book. **Attr.**

Parker, Dorothy **(1893–1967)** *American poet, writer, critic and wit*

This is not a novel to be tossed aside lightly. It should be thrown with great force. **In Gaines, Wit's End**

On A. A. Milne's The House at Pooh Corner *in her column 'Constant Reader'*
Tonstant Weader fwowed up. **The New Yorker, 1928**

Reger, Max **(1873–1916)** *German composer*

...YOU ARE WELCOME TO DO THE SAME WITH
THIS POWDERED GLASS IMPREGNATED LETTER.
YOURS, MAX.

Letter written to Rudolf Louis in response to his criticism of Reger's Sinfonietta, 1906
Ich sitze in dem kleinsten Zimmer in meinem Hause. Ich habe Ihre Kritik vor mir. Im nächsten Augenblick wird sie hinter mir sein.
[I am sitting in the smallest room in my house. I have your review in front of me. In a moment it will be behind me.]
In Slonimsky, The Lexicon of Musical Invective

Shaw, George Bernard **(1856–1950)** *Irish dramatist and critic*

A dramatic critic ... leaves no turn unstoned. **The New York Times, 1950**

Smith, Sydney **(1771–1845)** *English clergyman, essayist and wit*

I never read a book before reviewing it; it prejudices a man so.

In Pearson, The Smith of Smiths (1934)

Steinbeck, John **(1902–1968)** *American novelist*

On critics

Unless the bastards have the courage to give you unqualified praise, I say ignore them. **In J.K. Galbraith, A Life in Our Times (1981)**

Voltaire **(1694–1778)** *French author and critic*

Reviewing Rousseau's poem 'Ode to Posterity', c. 1778

I do not think this poem will reach its destination. **Attr.**

Wilde, Oscar **(1854–1900)** *Irish dramatist, novelist, critic and wit*

On a notice at a dancing saloon

I saw the only rational method of art criticism I have ever come across ... 'Please do not shoot the pianist. He is doing his best.'

'Impressions of America' (1906)

CURIOSITY

Bax, Sir Arnold **(1883–1953)** *English composer of romantic works*

One should try everything once, except incest and folk-dancing.

Carroll, Lewis **(1832–1898)** *English mathematician and children's novelist*

'If everybody minded their own business,' said the Duchess in a hoarse growl, 'the world would go round a deal faster than it does.'

Alice's Adventures in Wonderland (1865)

Graham, Harry **(1874–1936)** *British writer and journalist*

O'er the rugged mountain's brow
Clara threw the twins she nursed,
And remarked, 'I wonder now
Which will reach the bottom first?'

Ruthless Rhymes for Heartless Homes (1899), 'Calculating Clara'

Perelman, S.J. **(1904–1979)** *American humorist and writer*

Giving his reasons for refusing to see a priest as he lay dying
I am curious to see what happens in the next world to one who dies unshriven. **Attr.**

DEATH

Allen, Woody **(1935–)** *American film director, writer, actor and comedian*

It's not that I'm afraid to die. I just don't want to be there when it happens. **Without Feathers (1976)**

Anonymous

I feel no pain dear mother now
But oh, I am so dry!
O take me to a brewery
And leave me there to die.

Parody of Edward Farmer, 'The Collier's Dying Child'

Auber, Daniel (1782–1871) *French composer*

Remark made at a funeral
This is the last time I will take part as an amateur. **Attr.**

Austen, Jane (1775–1817) *English novelist*

We met … Dr Hall in such very deep mourning that either his mother, his wife, or himself must be dead. **Letter to Cassandra Austen, 1799**

Bowra, Sir Maurice (1898–1971) *English classical scholar*

Any amusing deaths lately? **Attr.**

Butler, Samuel (1835–1902) *English novelist, painter and philosopher*

When you have told anyone you have left him a legacy the only decent thing to do is to die at once. **In Festing Jones, Samuel Butler: A Memoir**

Chesterfield, Lord (1694–1773) *English politician, statesman, letter writer and orator*

Said when Tyrawley was old and infirm
Tyrawley and I have been dead these two years; but we don't choose to have it known. **In Boswell, The Life of Samuel Johnson (1791)**

Darrow, Clarence (1857–1938) *American lawyer, reformer and writer*

I have never killed a man, but I have read many obituaries with a lot of pleasure. **Medley**

Day, Clarence Shepard **(1874–1935)** *American essayist and humorist*

'If you don't go to other men's funerals,' he told Father stiffly, 'they won't go to yours.' **Life with Father (1935), 'Father plans'**

Edgeworth, Maria **(1767–1849)** *English-born Irish writer*

I've a great fancy to see my own funeral afore I die. **Attr.**

Henley, William Ernest **(1849–1903)** *English poet and playwright*

Madam Life's a piece in bloom
Death goes dogging everywhere:
She's the tenant of the room,
He's the ruffian on the stair. **Echoes (1877)**

Leacock, Stephen **(1869–1944)** *Canadian humorist and economist*

I detest life-insurance agents; they always argue that I shall someday die, which is not so. **Literary Lapses (1910)**

Mankiewicz, Herman J. **(1897–1953)** *American journalist and screenwriter*

Of death

It is the only disease you don't look forward to being cured of.

Citizen Kane, film, 1941

Marx, Groucho **(1895–1977)** *American film comedian*

Either he's dead or my watch has stopped. **A Day at the Races, film, 1937**

Saki (Hector Hugh Munro) **(1870–1916)** *British journalist and writer*

Waldo is one of those people who would be enormously improved by death. **Beasts and Super-Beasts (1914), 'The Feast of Nemesis'**

Spooner, William **(1844–1930)** *English clergyman and university warden*

Poor soul, very sad; her late husband, you know, a very sad death – eaten by missionaries – poor soul! **In William Hayter, Spooner (1977)**

Twain, Mark **(1835–1910)** *American humorist and novelist*

The report of my death was an exaggeration. **Cable, 1897**

DEBT

Fox, Henry Stephen (1791–1846) *English diplomat*

Remark after an illness
I am so changed that my oldest creditors would hardly know me.
Quoted by Byron in a letter to John Murray, 1817

Mumford, Ethel (1878–1940) *American novelist, dramatist and humorist*

In the midst of life we are in debt. **Altogether New Cynic's Calendar (1907)**

Sheridan, Richard Brinsley (1751–1816) *Irish comic dramatist*

Handing one of his creditors an IOU
Thank God, that's settled.
In C. Shriner, Wit, Wisdom, and Foibles of the Great (1918)

After being refused a loan of £25 from a friend who asked him to repay the £500 he had already borrowed
My dear fellow, be reasonable; the sum you ask me for is a very considerable one, whereas I only ask you for twenty-five pounds. **Attr.**

To his tailor when he requested payment of a debt, or at least the interest on it
It is not my interest to pay the principal, nor my principle to pay the interest. **Attr.**

Ward, Artemus (1834–1867) *American humorist, journalist, editor and lecturer*

Let us all be happy, and live within our means, even if we have to borrer the money to do it with. **'Science and Natural History'**

Wilde, Oscar (1854–1900) *Irish dramatist, novelist, critic and wit*

Wilde was to be charged a large fee for an operation
'Ah, well, then,' said Oscar, 'I suppose that I shall have to die beyond my means.' **In R.H. Sherard, Life of Oscar Wilde (1906)**

Wodehouse, P.G. (1881–1975) *English novelist*

I don't owe a penny to a single soul – not counting tradesmen, of course. **My Man Jeeves (1919), 'Jeeves and the Hard-Boiled Egg'**

DECEPTION

Gay, John (1685–1732) *English poet, dramatist and librettist*

To cheat a man is nothing; but the woman must have fine parts indeed who cheats a woman! **The Beggar's Opera (1728)**

Henry, O. (1862–1910) *American writer*

It was beautiful and simple as all truly great swindles are. **'The Octopus Marooned' (1908)**

Thurber, James (1894–1961) *American humorist, writer and illustrator*

It is not so easy to fool little girls today as it used to be. **Fables for Our Time (1940)**

You can fool too many of the people too much of the time. **The New Yorker, 1939, 'The Owl Who Was God'**

DIPLOMATS

Pearson, Lester B. (1897–1972) *Canadian politician*

Diplomacy is letting someone else have your way. **The Observer, 1965**

Ustinov, Sir Peter (1921–) *English actor, dramatist, writer and wit*

A diplomat these days is nothing but a head-waiter who's allowed to sit down occasionally. **Romanoff and Juliet (1956)**

Wotton, Sir Henry (1568–1639) *English traveller, diplomat and poet*

Legatus est vir bonus peregre missus ad mentiendum rei publicae causa. [An ambassador is an honest man sent to lie abroad for the good of his country.] **Written in an album, 1606**

DRESS

Ashford, Daisy (1881–1972) *English child author*

You look rather rash my dear your colors dont quite match your face. **The Young Visiters (1919)**

Chanel, Coco **(1883–1971)** *French couturier*

On Dior's New Look

These are clothes by a man who doesn't know women, never had one and dreams of being one. **Scotland on Sunday, 1995**

Darrow, Clarence **(1857–1938)** *American lawyer, reformer and writer*

I go to a better tailor than any of you and pay more for my clothes. The only difference is that you probably don't sleep in yours.

In E. Fuller, 2500 Anecdotes

Farquhar, George **(1678–1707)** *Irish comic dramatist*

A lady, if undrest at Church, looks silly,
One cannot be devout in dishabilly. **The Stage Coach (1704), Prologue**

Leacock, Stephen **(1869–1944)** *Canadian humorist and economist*

The general idea, of course, in any first-class laundry is to see that no shirt or collar ever comes back twice. **Winnowed Wisdom (1926)**

Nash, Ogden **(1902–1971)** *American humorous poet*

There was a young belle of old Natchez
Whose garments were always in patchez.
When comment arose
On the state of her clothes,
She drawled, When Ah itchez, Ah scratchez!

I'm a Stranger Here Myself (1935), 'Requiem'

Sure, deck your lower limbs in pants;
Yours are the limbs, my sweeting.
You look divine as you advance –
Have you seen yourself retreating?

The Face is Familiar (1940), 'What's the Use?'

Parker, Dorothy **(1893–1967)** *American poet, writer, critic and wit*

Where's the man could ease a heart,
Like a satin gown? **'The Satin Dress' (1937)**

Brevity is the soul of lingerie. **In Woollcott, While Rome Burns (1934)**

West, Mae **(1892–1980)** *American actress and scriptwriter*

You can say what you like about long dresses, but they cover a multitude of shins. **In J. Weintraub, Peel Me a Grape (1975)**

Whitehorn, Katherine **(1926–)** *English journalist and writer*

Hats divide generally into three classes: offensive hats, defensive hats, and shrapnel. **Shouts and Murmurs (1963), 'Hats'**

Wilde, Oscar **(1854–1900)** *Irish dramatist, novelist, critic and wit*

A well-tied tie is the first serious step in life.

A Woman of No Importance (1893)I

Wodehouse, P.G. **(1881–1975)** *English novelist*

The Right Hon was a tubby little chap who looked as if he had been poured into his clothes and had forgotten to say 'When!'

Very Good, Jeeves (1930), 'Jeeves and the Impending Doom'

ECONOMICS

Bagehot, Walter **(1826–1877)** *English economist and journalist*

No real English gentleman, in his secret soul, was ever sorry for the death of a political economist.

Estimates of some Englishmen and Scotchmen (1858)

Galbraith, J.K. **(1908–)** *Canadian-born American economist and author*

Economics is extremely useful as a form of employment for economists. **Attr.**

George, Eddie **(1938–)** *English banker*

There are three kinds of economist. Those who can count and those who can't. **The Observer Review, 1996**

Sellar, Walter **(1898–1951)** and **Yeatman, Robert** **(1897–1968)** *British humorous writers*

The National Debt is a very Good Thing and it would be dangerous to pay it off, for fear of Political Economy. **1066 And All That (1930)**

Shaw, George Bernard **(1856–1950)** *Irish dramatist and critic*

If all economists were laid end to end, they would not reach a conclusion. **Attr.**

Truman, Harry S. **(1884–1972)** *US President 1945–53*

It's a recession when your neighbour loses his job; it's a depression when you lose your own. **The Observer, 'Sayings of the Week', 1958**

Give me a one-handed economist! All my economists say, 'on the one hand ... on the other'. **In P. Boller, Presidential Anecdotes**

EDUCATION

Ade, George **(1866–1944)** *American fabulist and playwright*

'Whom are you?' said he, for he had been to night school. **Attr.**

Archibald, John Feltham **(1856–1919)** *Australian journalist*

I have nothing against Oxford men. Some of our best shearers' cooks are Oxford men. **In R. H. Croll, I Recall ...**

Bierce, Ambrose **(1842–c. 1914)** *American writer, journalist and soldier*

Education: That which discloses to the wise and disguises from the foolish their lack of understanding. **The Cynic's Word Book (1906)**

Cody, Henry John **(1868–1951)** *Canadian clergyman and educator*

Education is casting false pearls before real swine. **Attr.**

Moravia, Alberto **(1907–1990)** *Italian novelist*

The ratio of literacy to illiteracy is constant, but nowadays the illiterates can read and write. **The Observer, 1979**

Parker, Dorothy **(1893–1967)** *American poet, writer, critic and wit*

You can't teach an old dogma new tricks. **In James R. Gaines, Wit's End**

Saki (Hector Hugh Munro) **(1870–1916)** *British journalist and writer*

But, good gracious, you've got to educate him first. You can't expect a boy to be vicious till he's been to a good school.

Reginald in Russia (1910), 'The Baker's Dozen'

Searle, Ronald (1920–) *English cartoonist*

Though loaded firearms were strictly forbidden at St Trinian's to all but Sixth-Formers ... one or two of them carried automatics acquired in the holidays, generally the gift of some indulgent relative.

The Terror of St Trinian's (1952)

Maidens of St Trinian's
Gird your armour on.
Grab the nearest weapon
Never mind which one!
The battle's to the strongest
Might is always right,
Trample on the weakest
Glory in their plight!

'St Trinian's School Song', words by Sidney Gilliat

Sellar, Walter (1898–1951) and **Yeatman, Robert** (1897–1968)
British humorous writers

Do not on any account attempt to write on both sides of the paper at once.

1066 And All That (1930), Test Paper 5

For every person wishing to teach there are thirty not wanting to be taught.

And Now All This (1932),

Sitwell, Sir Osbert (1892–1969) *English author*

Educ: during the holidays from Eton.

Who's Who (1929)

Spooner, William (1844–1930) *English clergyman and university warden*

Sir, you have tasted two whole worms; you have hissed all my mystery lectures and have been caught fighting a liar in the quad; you will leave Oxford by the town drain.

Attr.

Spring-Rice, Cecil Arthur (1859–1918) *English diplomat*

I am the Dean of Christ Church, Sir:
There's my wife; look well at her.
She's the Broad and I'm the High;
We are the University.

In Hiscock (ed.), The Balliol Rhymes (1939), 'The Masque of Balliol'

Trapp, Joseph (1679–1747) *English poet, pamphleteer and clergyman*

The King, observing with judicious eyes,
The state of both his universities,

To Oxford sent a troop of horse, and why?
That learned body wanted loyalty;
To Cambridge books, as very well discerning,
How much that loyal body wanted learning.

Epigram on George I's donation of Bishop Ely's Library to Cambridge University.

Twain, Mark (1835–1910) *American humorist and novelist*

Cauliflower is nothing but cabbage with a college education.

Pudd'nhead Wilson's Calendar (1894)

Ustinov, Sir Peter (1921–) *English actor, dramatist, writer and wit*

People at the top of the tree are those without qualifications to detain them at the bottom. **Attr**

EGOISM

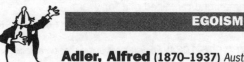

Adler, Alfred (1870–1937) *Austrian psychiatrist*

On hearing that an egocentric had fallen in love
Against whom? **Attr.**

Barnes, Peter (1931–) *English dramatist*

I know I am God because when I pray to him I find I'm talking to myself.

The Ruling Class (1968)

Bierce, Ambrose (1842–c. 1914) *American writer, journalist and soldier*

Egotist: A person of low taste, more interested in himself than in me.

The Cynic's Word Book (1906)

Bulmer-Thomas, Ivor (1905–1993) *Welsh politician*

Of Harold Wilson
If ever he went to school without any boots it was because he was too big for them. **Remark, 1949**

Sitwell, Dame Edith (1887–1964) *English poet, critic and biographer*

I have often wished I had time to cultivate modesty ... But I am too busy thinking about myself. **The Observer, 1950**

Whistler, James McNeill (1834–1903) *American painter and etcher*

Replying to the pointed observation that it was as well that we do not see ourselves as others see us

Isn't it? I know in my case I would grow intolerably conceited.

In Pearson, The Man Whistler

THE ENGLISH

Agate, James (1877–1947) *English dramatic critic and novelist*

The English instinctively admire any man who has no talent and is modest about it. **Attr.**

Behan, Brendan (1923–1964) *Irish author*

He was born an Englishman and remained one for years.

The Hostage (1958)

Betjeman, Sir John (1906–1984) *English poet and writer on architecture*

Think of what our Nation stands for,
Books from Boots' and country lanes,
Free speech, free passes, class distinction,
Democracy and proper drains.
Lord, put beneath Thy special care
One-eight-nine Cadogan Square.

Old Lights for New Chancels (1940), 'In Westminster Abbey'

Bradbury, Malcolm (1932–) *English novelist, critic and academic*

I like the English. They have the most rigid code of immorality in the world. **Eating People is Wrong (1954)**

Carlyle, Thomas (1795–1881) *Scottish historian and essayist*

When asked what the population of England was

Thirty millions, mostly fools. **Attr.**

MacInnes, Colin (1914–1976) *English author*

England is ... a country infested with people who love to tell us what to do, but who very rarely seem to know what's going on. **England, Half English**

Mikes, George **(1912–1987)** *Hungarian-born writer*

An Englishman, even if he is alone, forms an orderly queue of one.

How to be an Alien (1946)

Nash, Ogden **(1902–1971)** *American humorous poet*

Let us pause to consider the English
Who when they pause to consider themselves they get all reticently thrilled and tinglish.
Englishmen are distinguished by their traditions and ceremonials,
And also by their affection for their colonies and their condescension to their colonials.

Collected Works (1929), 'England Expects'

O'Connell, Daniel (1775–1847) *Irish nationalist politician*

The Englishman has all the qualities of a poker except its occasional warmth. **Attr.**

Smith, Sydney (1771–1845) *English clergyman, essayist and wit*

What a pity it is that we have no amusements in England but vice and religion! **In H. Pearson, The Smith of Smiths (1934)**

Sully, Duc de (1559–1641) *French financier*

Les Anglais s'amusent tristement, selon l'usage de leur pays.
[The English enjoy themselves sadly, according to the custom of their country.]
Memoirs (1638)

Tree, Sir Herbert Beerbohm (1853–1917) *English actor-manager*

The national sport of England is obstacle-racing. People fill their rooms with useless and cumbersome furniture, and spend the rest of their lives trying to dodge it. **In Hesketh Pearson, Beerbohm Tree (1956)**

Wilde, Oscar **(1854–1900)** *Irish dramatist, novelist, critic and wit*

The English have a miraculous power of turning wine into water. **Attr.**

EPITAPHS

Anonymous

Here lie I and my four daughters,
Killed by drinking Cheltenham waters.
Had we but stuck to Epsom salts,
We wouldn't have been in these here vaults. **'Cheltenham Waters'**

Here lie I by the chancel door;
They put me here because I was poor.
The further in, the more you pay,
But here lie I as snug as they. **Epitaph, Devon churchyard**

Here lies a man who was killed by lightning;
He died when his prospects seemed to be brightening.
He might have cut a flash in this world of trouble,
But the flash cut him, and he lies in the stubble.

Epitaph, Torrington, Devon

Here lies the body of Mary Ann Lowder,
She burst while drinking a seidlitz powder.
Called from the world to her heavenly rest,
She should have waited till it effervesced. **Epitaph**

Mary Ann has gone to rest,
Safe at last on Abraham's breast,
Which may be nuts for Mary Ann,
But is certainly rough on Abraham. **Epitaph**

Rest in peace – until we meet again.

Widow's epitaph for husband; in Mitford, The American Way of Death

Sacred to the memory of
Captain Anthony Wedgwood
Accidentally shot by his gamekeeper
Whilst out shooting
'Well done thou good and faithful servant'. **Epitaph**

Stranger! Approach this spot with gravity!
John Brown is filling his last cavity. **Epitaph of a dentist**

This is the grave of Mike O'Day
Who died maintaining his right of way.
His right was clear, his will was strong.
But he's just as dead as if he'd been wrong. **Epitaph**

Benchley, Robert **(1889–1945)** *American humorist and actor*

Suggesting an epitaph for an actress
She sleeps alone at last. **Attr.**

Bray, John Jefferson **(1912–)** *Australian lawyer and poet*

A hundred canvasses and seven sons
He left, and never got a likeness once. **'Epitaph on a Portrait Painter'**

Lockhart, John Gibson **(1794–1854)** *Scottish novelist and critic*

Here lies that peerless peer Lord Peter,
Who broke the laws of God and man and metre.

Epitaph for Patrick ('Peter'), Lord Robertson, 1890

EQUALITY

Balzac, Honoré de (1799–1850) *French novelist*

Equality may perhaps be a right, but no power on earth can ever turn it into a fact. **La Duchesse de Langeais (1834)**

Barrie, Sir J.M. (1860–1937) *Scottish novelist and dramatist*

His Lordship may compel us to be equal upstairs, but there will never be equality in the servants' hall. **The Admirable Crichton (1902)**

Gilbert, W.S. (1836–1911) *English librettist*

They all shall equal be!
The Earl, the Marquis, and the Dook,
The Groom, the Butler, and the Cook,
The Aristocrat who banks with Coutts,
The Aristocrat who cleans the boots. **The Gondoliers (1889)**

Huxley, Aldous (1894–1963) *English novelist*

That all men are equal is a proposition to which, at ordinary times, no sane human being has ever given his assent. **Proper Studies (1927)**

EXPERIENCE

Antrim, Minna (1861–1950) *American writer*

Experience is a good teacher, but she sends in terrific bills.

Naked Truth and Veiled Allusions (1902)

Fadiman, Clifton (1904–) *American writer, editor and broadcaster*

Experience teaches you that the man who looks you straight in the eye, particularly if he adds a firm handshake, is hiding something.

Enter, Conversing

Wilde, Oscar (1854–1900) *Irish dramatist, novelist, critic and wit*

Experience is the name every one gives to their mistakes.

Lady Windermere's Fan (1892)

FAME

Allen, Fred **(1894–1956)** *American comedian*

GOOD HEAVENS!
IS THAT
FLINT LOCKWEED
THE MOVIE STAR?

A celebrity is a person who works hard all his life to become known, then wears dark glasses to avoid being recognized. **Attr.**

Berners, Lord **(1883–1950)** *English composer, artist and novelist*

Of T.E. Lawrence
He's always backing into the limelight. **Attr.**

Cope, Wendy **(1945–)** *English writer and poet*

Response to an Engineering Council advertisement which asked why there was no Engineers' Corner in Westminster Abbey

Yes, life is hard if you choose engineering –
We make more fuss of ballads than of blueprints –
That's why so many poets end up rich,
While engineers scrape by in cheerless garrets.
Who needs a bridge or dam? Who needs a ditch? ...
Yes, life is hard if you choose engineering –
You're sure to need another job as well;
You'll have to plan your projects in the evenings
Instead of going out. It must be hell.

Making Cocoa for Kingsley Amis (1986), 'Engineers' Corner'

Peck, Gregory **(1916–)** *American actor*

On the fact that no-one in a crowded restaurant recognized him
If you have to tell them who you are, you aren't anybody.

In Harris, Pieces of Eight

Wilde, Oscar **(1854–1900)** *Irish dramatist, novelist, critic and wit*

There is only one thing in the world worse than being talked about, and that is not being talked about. **The Picture of Dorian Gray (1891)**

FAMILIES

Allen, Woody **(1935–)** *American film director, writer, actor and comedian*

And my parents finally realize that I'm kidnapped and they snap into action immediately: they rent out my room.

In Eric Lax, Woody Allen (1991)

Beerbohm, Sir Max **(1872–1956)** *English writer and caricaturist*

They were a tense and peculiar family, the Oedipuses, weren't they?

Attr.

Hubbard, Kin **(1868–1930)** *US caricaturist and humorist*

The old-time mother who used to wonder where her boy was now has a grandson who wonders where his mother is. **Attr.**

Humphries, Barry **(1934–)** *Australian entertainer*

Look at Patty Hearst. Those parents of hers cutting those peanut butter sandwiches day after day just to turn her into an urban guerilla!

In A Nice Night's Entertainment (1981)

Jewish proverb

God could not be everywhere, so therefore he made mothers.

Leacock, Stephen **(1869–1944)** *Canadian humorist and economist*

The parent who could see his boy as he really is, would shake his head and say: 'Willie is no good: I'll sell him.'

Essays and Literary Studies (1916), 'The Lot of a Schoolmaster'

Marx, Groucho **(1895–1977)** *American film comedian*

You're a disgrace to our family name of Wagstaff, if such a thing is possible. **Horse Feathers, 1932**

Nash, Ogden **(1902–1971)** *American humorous poet*

One would be in less danger
From the wiles of a stranger
If one's own kin and kith
Were more fun to be with. **Hard Lines (1931), 'Family Court'**

You two can be what you like, but since I am the big fromage in this family, I prefer to think of myself as the Gorgon Zola.

The Private Dining Room (1952), 'Medusa and the Mot Juste'

Scott-Maxwell, Florida **(1884–1979)**

No matter how old a mother is, she watches her middle-aged children for signs of improvement. **The Measure of My Days (1968)**

Thackeray, William Makepeace **(1811–1863)** *English novelist*

If a man's character is to be abused, say what you will, there's nobody like a relation to do the business. **Vanity Fair (1847–1848)**

Turnbull, Margaret **(fl. 1920s–1942)** *American author*

No man is responsible for his father. That is entirely his mother's affair.

Alabaster Lamps (1925)

Thurber, James **(1894–1961)** *American humorist, writer and illustrator*

Old Nat Burge sat ... watching the moon come up lazily out of the old cemetery in which nine of his daughters were lying, and only two of them were dead. **Let Your Mind Alone (1937), 'Bateman Comes Home'**

Twain, Mark **(1835–1910)** *American humorist and novelist*

When I was a boy of 14 my father was so ignorant I could hardly stand to have the old man around. But when I got to be 21, I was astonished at how much he had learned in seven years.

In Alan L. Mackay, The Harvest of a Quiet Eye (1977)

Whistler, James McNeill **(1834–1903)** *American painter and etcher*

Explaining to a snobbish lady why he had been born in such an unfashionable place as Lowell, Massachusetts

The explanation is quite simple. I wished to be near my mother. **Attr.**

Wodehouse, P.G. **(1881–1975)** *English novelist*

It is no use telling me that there are bad aunts and good aunts. At the core they are all alike. Sooner or later, out pops the cloven hoof.

The Code of the Woosters (1938)

FATE

Beerbohm, Sir Max **(1872–1956)** *English writer and caricaturist*

Of Queen Caroline

Fate wrote her a tremendous tragedy, and she played it in tights.

King George the Fourth

Hare, Maurice Evan **(1886–1967)** *English limerick writer*

There once was a man who said, 'Damn!
It is borne in upon me I am
An engine that moves
In predestinate grooves,
I'm not even a bus, I'm a tram.' **'Limerick', 1905**

Loos, Anita **(1893–1981)** *American humorous novelist and screenwriter*

Fate keeps on happening. **Gentlemen Prefer Blondes (1925)**

Simpson, N.F. **(1919–)** *English author and playwright*

Each of us as he receives his private trouncings at the hands of fate is kept in good heart by the moth in his brother's parachute, and the scorpion in his neighbour's underwear. **A Resounding Tinkle (1958)**

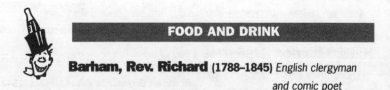

FOOD AND DRINK

Barham, Rev. Richard **(1788–1845)** *English clergyman and comic poet*

She help'd him to lean, and she help'd him to fat,
And it look'd like hare – but it might have been cat.

The Ingoldsby Legends (1840–1847), 'The Bagman's Dog'

Bowra, Sir Maurice **(1898–1971)** *English classical scholar*

I'm a man
More dined against than dining. **In J. Betjeman, Summoned by Bells (1960)**

Campbell, Mrs Patrick **(1865–1940)** *English actress*

To Bernard Shaw, a vegetarian
Some day you'll eat a pork chop, Joey, and then God help all women.
In Alexander Woollcott, While Rome Burns (1934)

Elizabeth, the Queen Mother **(1900–)**

Remark after a fishbone had lodged in her throat
The salmon are striking back. **Attr.**

Evarts, William Maxwell **(1818–1901)** *American lawyer and statesman*

Of a dinner given by US President and temperance advocate Rutherford B. Hayes
It was a brilliant affair; water flowed like champagne. **Attr.**

Fadiman, Clifton **(1904–)** *American writer, editor and broadcaster*

Cheese – milk's leap toward immortality. **Any Number Can Play (1957)**

Fields, W.C. **(1880–1946)** *American comic film actor*

His reason for not drinking water
Fish fuck in it. **Attr.**

Galsworthy, John **(1867–1933)** *English novelist*

The French cook; we open tins. **Treasury of Humorous Quotations**

Johnson, Samuel **(1709–1784)** *English lexicographer, poet and critic*

A cucumber should be well sliced, and dressed with pepper and vinegar, and then thrown out, as good for nothing.
In Boswell, Journal of a Tour to the Hebrides (1785)

Lutyens, Sir Edwin Landseer **(1869–1944)** *English architect*

Comment made in a restaurant
This piece of cod passes all understanding.
In Robert Lutyens, Sir Edwin Lutyens (1942)

Mankiewicz, Herman J. **(1897–1953)** *American journalist and screenwriter*

After being sick at the table of a fastidious host
It's all right, Arthur. The white wine came up with the fish. **Attr.**

Peter, Laurence J. (1919–1990) *Canadian author, educator and psychologist*

The noblest of all dogs is the hot-dog; it feeds the hand that bites it.

Quotations for Our Time (1977)

Piggy, Miss *Puppet character from The Muppets, created by Jim Henson*

Never eat anything at one sitting that you can't lift.

Woman's Hour, BBC Radio Programme, 1992

Portland, Sixth Duke of (1857–1943)

On being told to reduce his expenses by dispensing with one of his two Italian pastry cooks

What! Can't a fellow even enjoy a biscuit any more?

In Winchester, Their Noble Lordships

Punch *British humorous periodical, founded 1841*

'I'm afraid you've got a bad egg, Mr Jones.' 'Oh no, my Lord, I assure you! Parts of it are excellent!' **1895**

St Leger, Warham (1850–c. 1915) *English comic writer and librettist*

There is a fine stuffed chavender,
A chavender, or chub,
That decks the rural pavender,
The pavender, or pub,
Wherein I eat my gravender,
My gravender, or grub. **'The Chavender, or Chub'**

Saki (Hector Hugh Munro) (1870–1916) *British journalist and writer*

The cook was a good cook, as cooks go; and as cooks go she went.

Reginald (1904), 'Reginald on Besetting Sins'

Secombe, Sir Harry (1921–) *Welsh comedian and singer*

My advice if you insist on slimming: Eat as much as you like – just don't swallow it. **Daily Herald, 1962**

Smith, Sydney (1771–1845) *English clergyman, essayist and wit*

On his convalescent diet

If you hear of sixteen or eighteen pounds of human flesh, they belong to me. I look as if a curate has been taken out of me.

Letter to Lady Carlisle, 1844

Webster, John **(c. 1580–c. 1625)** *English dramatist*

I saw him even now going the way of all flesh, that is to say towards the kitchen. **Westward Hoe (1607)**

Wilde, Oscar **(1854–1900)** *Irish dramatist, novelist, critic and wit*

Said to Frank Harris who was listing the houses he had dined at
Dear Frank, we believe you; you have dined in every house in London – once. **Attr.**

Wodehouse, P.G. **(1881–1975)** *English novelist*

The lunches of fifty-seven years had caused his chest to slip down to the mezzanine floor. **The Heart of a Goof (1926), 'Chester Forgets Himself'**

FOOLS

Beecher, Henry Ward **(1813–1887)** *American clergyman and author*

On receiving a note containing only one word: 'Fool'
I have known many an instance of a man writing a letter and forgetting to sign his name, but this is the only instance I have ever known of a man signing his name and forgetting to write the letter. **Attr.**

Curtiz, Michael **(1888–1962)** *Hungarian film director*

The next time I send a damn fool for something, I go myself. **In Zierold, Moguls (1969)**

Pope, Alexander **(1688–1744)** *English poet, translator and editor*

Sir, I admit your gen'ral Rule
That every Poet is a Fool;
But you yourself may serve to show it,
That every Fool is not a Poet. **'Epigram from the French' (1732)**

Rowland, Helen **(1875–1950)** *American writer*

The follies which a man regrets most in his life are those which he didn't commit when he had the opportunity. **A Guide to Men (1922)**

Twain, Mark **(1835–1910)** *American humorist and novelist*

Hain't we got all the fools in town on our side? and ain't that a big enough majority in any town? **The Adventures of Huckleberry Finn (1884)**

FRIENDS

Bradbury, Malcolm **(1932–)** *English novelist, critic and academic*

I've noticed your hostility towards him ... I ought to have guessed you were friends. **The History Man (1975)**

Bulwer-Lytton, Edward George **(1803–1873)** *English diplomatist and author*

There is no man so friendless but what he can find a friend sincere enough to tell him disagreeable truths. **What Will He Do With It? (1857)**

Colette **(1873–1954)** *French novelist*

My true friends have always given me that supreme proof of devotion, a spontaneous aversion for the man I loved. **Break of Day (1928)**

Kingsmill, Hugh **(1889–1949)** *English biographer*

Friends are God's apology for relations. **In Ingrams, God's Apology (1977)**

Twain, Mark **(1835–1910)** *American humorist and novelist*

The holy passion of Friendship is of so sweet and steady and loyal and enduring a nature that it will last through a whole lifetime, if not asked to lend money. **Pudd'nhead Wilson's Calendar (1894)**

Vidal, Gore **(1925–)** *American novelist, dramatist, essayist, critic and poet*

Whenever a friend succeeds, a little something in me dies.

The Sunday Times Magazine, 1973.

GENIUS

GENIUS

Whistler, James McNeill **(1834–1903)** *American painter and etcher*

Replying to a lady inquiring whether he thought genius hereditary

I cannot tell you that, madam. Heaven has granted me no offspring.

In D.C. Seitz, Whistler Stories (1913)

Wilde, Oscar **(1854–1900)** *Irish dramatist, novelist, critic and wit*

At the New York Customs

I have nothing to declare except my genius. **In F. Harris, Oscar Wilde (1918)**

GENTLEMEN

Allen, Fred **(1894–1956)** *American comedian*

WHEN THE QUEEN SAYS 'HELLO', KEEP YOUR HAT ON!

A gentleman is any man who wouldn't hit a woman with his hat on. **Attr**

Ashford, Daisy (1881–1972) *English child author*

I do hope I shall enjoy myself with you ... I am parshial to ladies if they are nice I suppose it is my nature. I am not quite a gentleman but you would hardly notice it. **The Young Visiters (1919)**

Benchley, Robert (1889–1945) *American humorist and actor*

Even nowadays a man can't step up and kill a woman without feeling just a bit unchivalrous. **Attr.**

Chifley, Joseph Benedict (1885–1951) *Australian politician*

My experience of gentlemen's agreements is that, when it comes to the pinch, there are rarely enough bloody gentlemen about.

In Crisp, Ben Chifley (1960)

Surtees, R.S. (1805–1864) *English journalist and novelist*

The only infallible rule we know is, that the man who is always talking about being a gentleman never is one. **Ask Mamma (1858)**

GOD

Allen, Woody (1935–) *American film director, writer, actor and comedian*

Not only is there no God, but try getting a plumber on weekends.

Getting Even (1971), 'My Philosophy'

Of God

The worst that can be said is that he's an under-achiever.

Love and Death, film, 1976

If only God would give me some clear sign! Like making a large deposit in my name at a Swiss bank. **Without Feathers (1976)**

Ewer, William Norman (1885–1976) *English journalist*

How odd
Of God
To choose
The Jews. **In Week-End Book (1924), 'How Odd'**

Browne, Cecil **(1932–)** *American businessman*

But not so odd
As those who choose
A Jewish God,
But spurn the Jews.

Reply to William Norman Ewer: How odd/Of God/To choose/The Jews

Haldane, J.B.S. **(1892–1964)** *Anglo-Indian biologist*

Reply when asked what inferences could be drawn about the nature of God from a study of his works

The Creator ... has a special preference for beetles. **Lecture, 1951**

Hughes, Sean **(1966–)** *Irish comedian*

I'd like to thank God for fucking up my life and at the same time not existing, quite a special skill. **The Independent, 1993**

Knox, Ronald **(1888–1957)** *English Roman Catholic priest and theologian*

There was once a man who said 'God
Must think it exceedingly odd
If he finds that this tree
Continues to be
When there's no one about in the Quad.' **Attr.**

Anonymous

Dear Sir, Your astonishment's odd:
I am always about in the Quad.
And that's why the tree
Will continue to be,
Since observed by Yours faithfully, God.

Reply to Ronald Knox, 'There was once a man'

Squire, Sir J.C. **(1884–1958)** *English poet, writer and critic*

God heard the embattled nations sing and shout
'Gott strafe England!' and 'God save the King!'
God this, God that, and God the other thing –
'Good God!' said God, 'I've got my work cut out.'

The Survival of the Fittest (1916), 'Epigrams: 1, The Dilemma'

Woollcott, Alexander (1887–1943) *American journalist and critic*

On being shown round Moss Hart's elegant country house and grounds
Just what God would have done if he had the money. **Attr.**

GOSSIP

Bierce, Ambrose (1842–c.1914) *American writer, journalist and soldier*

Backbite: To speak of a man as you find him when he can't find you.

The Enlarged Devil's Dictionary (1961)

Congreve, William (1670–1729) *English dramatist and poet*

They come together like the Coroner's Inquest, to sit upon the murdered reputations of the week. **The Way of the World (1700)**

Farquhar, George (1678–1707) *Irish comic dramatist*

I believe they talked of me, for they laughed consumedly.

The Beaux' Stratagem (1707)

Ingham, Bernard (1932–) *English journalist and civil servant*

Blood sport is brought to its ultimate refinement in the gossip columns.

Remark, 1986

Longworth, Alice Roosevelt (1884–1980) *American author, hostess and wit*

Embroidered on a cushion at her home in Washington
If you haven't anything nice to say about anyone, come and sit by me.

New York Times, 1980

Russell, Bertrand (1872–1970) *Welsh philosopher, mathematician and author*

No one gossips about other people's secret virtues.

On Education, especially in early childhood (1926)

Sheridan, Richard Brinsley (1751–1816) *Irish comic dramatist*

Here is the whole set! a character dead at every word.

The School for Scandal (1777)

GOVERNMENT

Burns, George **(1896–1996)** *American comedian*

Too bad all the people who know how to run the country are busy driving cabs and cutting hair. **Attr.**

Giles, Geoffrey O'Halloran **(1923–)**

The Government, in due course, acted promptly. **Age, 1982**

Rogers, Will **(1879–1935)** *American comic actor, rancher, writer and wit*

I don't make jokes – I just watch the government and report the facts. **Attr.**

HAPPINESS

Shaw, George Bernard **(1856–1950)** *Irish dramatist and critic*

A lifetime of happiness! No man alive could bear it: it would be hell on earth. **Man and Superman (1903)**

Waugh, Evelyn **(1903–1966)** *English journalist and novelist*

I can't quite explain it, but I don't believe one can ever be unhappy for long provided one does just exactly what one wants to and when one wants to. **Decline and Fall (1928)**

HATRED

De Vries, Peter **(1910–1993)** *American novelist and humorist*

Everybody hates me because I'm so universally liked.

The Vale of Laughter (1967)

Fields, W.C. **(1880–1946)** *American comic film actor*

I am free of all prejudice. I hate everyone equally. **Attr.**

Gabor, Zsa-Zsa **(1919–)** *Hungarian film actress*

I never hated a man enough to give him his diamonds back.

The Observer, 'Sayings of the Week', 1957

Nash, Ogden **(1902–1971)** *American humorous poet*

Any kiddie in school can love like a fool,
But hating, my boy, is an art.

Happy Days (1933), 'Plea for Less Malice Toward None'

Rosten, Leo **(1908–1997)** *American social scientist, writer and humorist*

Of W.C. Fields; often attributed to him

Any man who hates dogs and babies can't be all bad.

Speech, Masquer's Club dinner, 1939

HISTORY

Balfour, A.J. **(1848–1930)** *Scottish statesman*

History does not repeat itself. Historians repeat each other. **Attr.**

Eban, Abba **(1915–)** *Israeli diplomat and politician*

History teaches us that men and nations behave wisely once they have exhausted all other alternatives. **Speech, 1970**

Lang, Ian **(1940–)** *Scottish Conservative politician*

History is littered with dead opinion polls. **The Independent, 1994**

Saki (Hector Hugh Munro) **(1870–1916)** *British journalist and writer*

The people of Crete unfortunately make more history than they can consume locally.

The Chronicles of Clovis (1911), 'The Jesting of Arlington Stringham'

Taylor, A.J.P. **(1906–1990)** *English historian*

Of Napoleon III

He was what I often think is a dangerous thing for a statesman to be – a student of history; and like most of those who study history, he learned from the mistakes of the past how to make new ones.

The Listener, 1963

Tolstoy, Leo **(1828–1910)** *Russian writer*

Historians are like deaf people who go on answering questions that no one has asked them. **Attr.**

HOME

Ace, Jane **(1905–1974)**

Home wasn't built in a day. **In G. Ace, The Fine Art of Hypochondria (1966)**

Anonymous

Be it ever so humble there's no place like home for sending one slowly crackers. **Obiter Dicta**

There's no place like home, after the other places close.

Fletcher, John **(1579–1625)**

Charity and beating begins at home. **Wit Without Money (c.1614)**

Shaw, George Bernard **(1856–1950)** *Irish dramatist and critic*

The great advantage of a hotel is that it's a refuge from home life.

You Never Can Tell (1898)

HONOUR

Graham, Harry **(1874–1936)** *British writer and journalist*

Weep not for little Léonie
Abducted by a French Marquis!

Though loss of honour was a wrench
Just think how it's improved her French.

More Ruthless Rhymes for Heartless Homes (1930), 'Compensation'

Marx, Groucho (1895–1977) *American film comedian*

Remember, men, we're fighting for this woman's honour; which is probably more than she ever did. **Duck Soup, film, 1933**

Twain, Mark (1835–1910) *American humorist and novelist*

The cross of the Legion of Honour has been conferred upon me. However, few escape that distinction. **A Tramp Abroad (1880)**

HUMAN NATURE

Allen, Woody (1935–) *American film director, writer, actor and comedian*

More than any other time in history, mankind faces a crossroads. One path leads to despair and utter hopelessness. The other, to total extinction. Let us pray we have the wisdom to choose correctly.

Side Effects, 'My Speech to the Graduates'

Beerbohm, Sir Max (1872–1956) *English writer and caricaturist*

Mankind is divisible into two great classes: hosts and guests. **Attr.**

Donleavy, J.P. (1926–) *American-born Irish author*

I got disappointed in human nature as well and gave it up because I found it too much like my own. **Fairy Tales of New York (1961)**

Marquis, Don (1878–1937) *American columnist, satirist and poet*

Ours is a world where people don't know what they want and are willing to go through hell to get it. **In Treasury of Humorous Quotations**

O'Brien, Flann (1911–1966) *Irish novelist and journalist*

The pocket was the first instinct of humanity and was used long years before the human race had a trousers between them – the quiver for arrows is one example and the pocket of the kangaroo is another.

At Swim-Two-Birds (1939)

O'Rourke, P.J. (1947–) *American writer and humorist*

There are two kinds of people in the world: those who believe there are two kinds of people in the world, and those who don't. **Attr.**

Schulz, Charles (1922–) *American cartoonist*

I love mankind – it's people I can't stand. **Go Fly a Kite, Charlie Brown**

Twain, Mark (1835–1910) *American humorist and novelist*

Man is the Only Animal that Blushes. Or needs to.

Following the Equator (1897)

HUMOUR

Barker, Ronnie (1929–) *English comedian*

The marvellous thing about a joke with a double meaning is that it can only mean one thing. **Attr.**

Berlin, Irving (1888–1989) *Russian-born American songwriter*

Telegram message to Groucho Marx on his seventy-first birthday

The world would not be in such a snarl, had Marx been Groucho instead of Karl. **Attr.**

Dodd, Ken (1931–) *English comedian*

On Freud's theory that a good joke will lead to great relief and elation
The trouble with Freud is that he never played the Glasgow Empire Saturday night after Rangers and Celtic had both lost. **TV interview, 1965**

Rogers, Will (1879–1935) *American comic actor, rancher, writer and wit*

Everything is funny as long as it is happening to someone else.
The Illiterate Digest (1924)

Wodehouse, P.G. (1881–1975) *English novelist*

She had a penetrating sort of laugh. Rather like a train going into a tunnel. **The Inimitable Jeeves (1923)**

IDLENESS

Nash, Ogden (1902–1971) *American humorous poet*

I would live my life in nonchalance and insouciance
Were it not for making a living, which is rather a nouciance.
The Face is Familiar (1940), 'Introspective Reflection'

Sheridan, Richard Brinsley (1751–1816) *Irish comic dramatist*

On a notice fixed to his door when he was a Secretary to the Treasury
No applications can be received here on Sundays, nor any business done during the remainder of the week.

Attr. in Morwood, The Life and Works of Richard Brinsley Sheridan (1985)

Thurber, James (1894–1961) *American humorist, writer and illustrator*

It is better to have loafed and lost than never to have loafed at all.

Fables for Our Time (1940)

Ward, Artemus (1834–1867) *American humorist, journalist, editor and lecturer*

I am happiest when I am idle. I could live for months without performing any kind of labour, and at the expiration of that time I should feel fresh and vigorous enough to go right on in the same way for numerous more months. **Artemus Ward in London (1867)**

ILLNESS

Aubrey, John (1626–1697) *English antiquary*

Sciatica: he cured it, by boiling his buttock.

Brief Lives (c. 1693), 'Sir Jonas Moore'

Austin, Alfred (1835–1913) *English poet*

On the illness of the Prince of Wales
Across the wires the electric message came:
'He is no better, he is much the same.' **Attr.**

Benny, Jack (1894–1974) *American comedian*

Said on receiving an award
I don't deserve this, but I have arthritis, and I don't deserve that either. **Attr.**

Fields, W.C. (1880–1946) *American comic film actor*

The best cure for insomnia is to get a lot of sleep. **Attr.**

Heller, Joseph (1923–) *American novelist*

Hungry Joe collected lists of fatal diseases and arranged them in alphabetical order so that he could put his finger without delay on any one he wanted to worry about. **Catch-22 (1961)**

McAuley, James Philip **(1917–1976)** *Australian poet and critic*

After his first cancer operation; to a friend
Well, better a semi-colon than a full stop!

In Peter Coleman, The Heart of James McAuley (1980)

Parker, Dorothy **(1893–1967)** *American poet, writer, critic and wit*

Pressing a button marked NURSE during a stay in hospital
That should assure us of at least forty-five minutes of undisturbed privacy. **In Gaines, Days and Nights of the Algonquin Round Table (1977)**

Perelman, S.J. **(1904–1979)** *American humorist, journalist and dramatist*

I've got Bright's disease and he's got mine. **Attr.**

Ward, Artemus **(1834–1867)** *American humorist; journalist, editor and lecturer*

Did you ever have the measels, and if so how many?

Artemus Ward, His Book (1862), 'The Census'

IMMORTALITY

Allen, Woody **(1935–)** *American film director, writer, actor and comedian*

I don't want to achieve immortality through my work ... I want to achieve it by not dying. **Attr.**

Ertz, Susan **(1894–1985)** *English writer*

Someone has somewhere commented on the fact that millions long for immortality who don't know what to do with themselves on a rainy Sunday afternoon. **Anger in the Sky (1943)**

Galbraith J.K. **(1908–)** *Canadian-born American economist and author*

If all else fails, immortality can always be assured by spectacular error. **Attr.**

Heller, Joseph **(1923–)** *American novelist*

He had decided to live forever or die in the attempt. **Catch-22 (1961)**

INDECISION

Asquith, Margot **(1864–1945)** *Scottish political hostess and writer*

Of Sir Stafford Cripps

He has a brilliant mind until he makes it up. **In The Wit of the Asquiths**

Nash, Ogden **(1902–1971)** *American humorous poet*

If I could but spot a conclusion, I should race to it. **The Private Dining Room (1952)**

Smith, Sir Cyril **(1928–)** *British Liberal politician*

If the fence is strong enough I'll sit on it. **The Observer, 1974**

Twain, Mark **(1835–1910)** *American humorist and novelist*

I must have a prodigious quantity of mind; it takes me as much as a week, sometimes, to make it up. **The Innocents Abroad (1869)**

THE IRISH

Anonymous

Ah well, they say it's not as bad as they say it is.

An Irish woman's view on the situation in Ulster

Behan, Brendan (1923–1964) *Irish author*

Pat: He was an Anglo-Irishman.
Meg: In the blessed name of God, what's that?
Pat: A Protestant with a horse. **The Hostage (1958)**

Other people have a nationality. The Irish and the Jews have a psychosis. **Richard's Cork Leg**

KNOWLEDGE

Beeching, Rev. H.C. **(1859–1919)** *English theologian, preacher and poet*

First come I; my name is Jowett.
There's no knowledge but I know it.
I am Master of this college:
What I don't know isn't knowledge. **'The Masque of Balliol' (late 1870s)**

Monsarrat, Nicholas **(1910–1979)** *British novelist*

You English ... think we know damn nothing but I tell you we know damn all. **The Cruel Sea (1951)**

Mumford, Ethel **(1878–1940)** *American novelist, dramatist and humorist*

Knowledge is power if you know it about the right person.

In Cowan, The Wit of Women

Sharpe, Tom **(1928–)** *English comic novelist*

His had been an intellectual decision founded on his conviction that if a little knowledge was a dangerous thing, a lot was lethal.

Porterhouse Blue (1974)

Sheridan, Richard Brinsley **(1751–1816)** *Irish comic dramatist*

Madam, a circulating library in a town is an ever-green tree of diabolical knowledge! – It blossoms through the year! – And depend on it, Mrs Malaprop, that they who are so fond of handling the leaves, will long for the fruit at last. **The Rivals (1775)**

LANGUAGE

Churchill, Sir Winston **(1874–1965)** *English statesman*

Marginal comment on a document

This is the sort of English up with which I will not put.

In Gowers, Plain Words (1948)

SAY, IS THIS LOOGABAROOGA?
LOUGHBOROUGH

Everybody has a right to pronounce foreign names as he chooses.

The Observer, 1951

Day, Clarence Shepard (1874–1935) *American essayist and humorist*

Imagine the Lord talking French! Aside from a few odd words in Hebrew, I took it completely for granted that God had never spoken anything but the most dignified English. **Life with Father (1935)**

Dickens, Charles (1812–1870) *English author*

There was no light nonsense about Miss Blimber ... She was dry and sandy with working in the graves of deceased languages. None of your live languages for Miss Blimber. They must be dead – stone dead – and then Miss Blimber dug them up like a Ghoul. **Dombey and Son (1848)**

Goldwyn, Samuel (1882–1974) *Polish-born American film producer*

Let's have some new clichés. **The Observer, 'Sayings of the Week', 1948**

Knox, Ronald (1888–1957) *English Roman Catholic priest and theologian*

Said when asked to conduct a baptism service in English

The baby doesn't understand English and the Devil knows Latin.

In Evelyn Waugh, Ronald Knox, I, 5

Schleiermacher, F.E.D. **(1768–1834)** *German Protestant theologian*

Of a celebrated philologist
He could be silent in seven languages. **Attr.**

Shaw, George Bernard **(1856–1950)** *Irish dramatist and critic*

England and America are two countries separated by the same language. **Reader's Digest, 1942**

Sheridan, Richard Brinsley **(1751–1816)** *Irish comic dramatist*

An aspersion upon my parts of speech! … If I reprehend anything in this world, it is the use of my oracular tongue, and a nice derangement of epitaphs! **The Rivals (1775)**

Skelton, Robin **(1925–)** *Canadian critic, editor and poet*

Anything said off the cuff has usually been written on it first. **Attr.**

Smith, F.E. **(1872–1930)** *English lawyer and statesman*

When the Labour MP J.H. Thomas complained he 'ad a 'eadache'
Try taking a couple of aspirates. **Attr.**

Tomlin, Lily **(1939–)** *American actress and comedian*

Man invented language in order to satisfy his deep need to complain.
In Pinker, The Language Instinct (1994)

Tucholsky, Kurt (1890–1935) *German satirist and writer*

Das Englische ist eine einfache, aber schwere Sprache. Es besteht aus lauter Fremdwörtern die falsch ausgesprochen werden. [English is a simple, yet hard language. It consists entirely of foreign words pronounced wrongly.]

Schnipsel (Scraps, 1973)

Twain, Mark (1835–1910) *American humorist and novelist*

They spell it Vinci and pronounce it Vinchy; foreigners always spell better than they pronounce. **The Innocents Abroad (1869)**

A verb has a hard time enough of it in this world when it's all together. It's downright inhuman to split it up. But that's just what those Germans do. They take part of a verb and put it down here, like a stake, and they take the other part of it and put it away over yonder like another stake, and between these two limits they just shovel in German.

Address at dinner of The Nineteenth Century Club, 1900

Waugh, Evelyn (1903–1966) *English journalist and novelist*

Cable sent after he had failed, while a journalist in Ethiopia, to substantiate a rumour that an English nurse had been blown up in an Italian air raid

Nurse unupblown. **In R. Claiborne, Our Marvellous Native Tongue**

Webster, Noah (1758–1843) *American lexicographer, teacher and writer*

Responding to his wife's comment that she had been surprised to find him embracing their maid

No, my dear, it is *I* who am surprised; you are merely astonished. **Attr.**

Weinreich, Professor Max

A language is a dialect that has an army and a navy.

In Rosten, The Joys of Yiddish (1968)

Whitehorn, Katherine (1926–) *English journalist and writer*

A good listener is not someone who has nothing to say. A good listener is a good talker with a sore throat. **Attr.**

Woollcott, Alexander (1887–1943) *American journalist and critic*

Subjunctive to the last, he preferred to ask, 'And that, sir, would be the Hippodrome?' **While Rome Burns (1934), 'Our Mrs Parker'**

LAW

Adams, Richard **(1846–1908)** *Irish journalist, barrister and judge*

You have been acquitted by a Limerick jury and you may now leave the dock without any other stain on your character.

In Maurice Healy, The Old Munster Circuit (1939)

Bentham, Jeremy **(1748–1832)** *English philosopher and jurist*

Lawyers are the only persons in whom ignorance of the law is not punished. **Attr.**

Bierce, Ambrose **(1842–c. 1914)** *American writer, journalist and soldier*

Lawsuit: A machine which you go into as a pig and come out as a sausage. **The Cynic's Word Book (1906)**

Holmes, Hugh **(1840–1916)** *Irish judge*

An elderly pensioner on being sentenced to fifteen years' penal servitude cried: 'Ah! my Lord, I'm a very old man, and I'll never do that sentence.' The judge replied 'Well try to do as much of it as you can.'

In Maurice Healy, The Old Munster Circuit (1939)

Kennedy, John F. **(1917–1963)** *US President, 1961–63*

On being criticized for making his brother Robert attorney general

I can't see that it's wrong to give him a little legal experience before he goes out to practise law. **In M. Ringo, Nobody Said It Better**

Knox, Philander Chase **(1853–1921)** *American diplomat and lawyer*

Reply when Theodore Roosevelt requested legal justification for US acquisition of the Panama Canal Zone

Oh, Mr President, do not let so great an achievement suffer from any taint of legality. **Attr.**

Maynard, Sir John **(1602–1690)** *English judge*

Reply to Judge Jeffreys' suggestion that he was so old he had forgotten the law

I have forgotten more law than you ever knew, but allow me to say, I have not forgotten much. **Attr.**

Smith, F.E. **(1872–1930)** *English lawyer and statesman*

Judge Willis: What do you suppose I am on the Bench for, Mr Smith?
F.E. Smith: It is not for me to attempt to fathom the inscrutable workings of Providence.

In Birkenhead, Frederick Elwin, Earl of Birkenhead (1933)

To a judge who complained that he was no wiser at the end than at the start of one of Smith's cases
Possibly not, My Lord, but far better informed.

In Birkenhead, Life of F.E. Smith (1959)

LIES

Anonymous

An abomination unto the Lord, but a very present help in time of trouble.

Definition of a lie

Asquith, Margot **(1864–1945)** *Scottish political hostess and writer*

Of Lady Desborough
She tells enough white lies to ice a wedding cake.

Quoted by Lady Violet Bonham Carter in The Listener, June 1953

Belloc, Hilaire **(1870–1953)** *French-born English writer and poet*

Matilda told such Dreadful Lies,
It made one Gasp and Stretch one's Eyes;

Her Aunt, who, from her Earliest Youth,
Had kept a Strict Regard for Truth,
Attempted to Believe Matilda:
The effort very nearly killed her. **Cautionary Tales (1907), 'Matilda'**

Beresford, Lord Charles **(1846–1919)** *English admiral and politician*

Very sorry can't come. Lie follows by post.

Telegram to the Prince of Wales in response to an eleventh-hour summons to dine

Butler, Samuel **(1835–1902)** *English novelist, painter and philosopher*

Any fool can tell the truth, but it requires a man of some sense to know how to lie well. **The Note-Books of Samuel Butler (1912)**

Maugham, William Somerset **(1874–1965)** *British writer*

She's too crafty a woman to invent a new lie when an old one will serve.

The Constant Wife (1927)

Saki (Hector Hugh Munro) **(1870–1916)** *British journalist and writer*

A little inaccuracy sometimes saves tons of explanation.

The Square Egg (1924)

Salmon, George **(1819–1904)** *Provost of Trinity College, Dublin*

Remark at the unveiling of a portrait of a colleague

Excellent, excellent, you can just hear the lies trickling out of his mouth.

Attr.

Sheridan, Richard Brinsley **(1751–1816)** *Irish comic dramatist*

On being asked to apologize for calling a fellow MP a liar

Mr Speaker, I said the honourable member was a liar it is true and I am sorry for it. The honourable member may place the punctuation where he pleases. **Attr.**

Twain, Mark **(1835–1910)** *American humorist and novelist*

There are three kinds of lies: lies, damned lies, and statistics.

Autobiography (1959 edition)

Vidal, Gore **(1925–)** *American novelist, dramatist, essayist, critic and poet*

He will lie even when it is inconvenient, the sign of the true artist.

Two Sisters (1970)

Wilde, Oscar **(1854–1900)** *Irish dramatist, novelist, critic and wit*

Untruthful! My nephew Algernon? Impossible! He is an Oxonian.

The Importance of Being Earnest (1895)

LIFE

Bennett, Alan **(1934–)** *English dramatist, actor and diarist*

You know life ... it's rather like opening a tin of sardines. We are all of us looking for the key.

Beyond the Fringe (1962)

Butler, Samuel **(1835–1902)** *English novelist, painter and philosopher*

Life is one long process of getting tired.

The Note-Books of Samuel Butler (1912)

Chaplin, Charlie **(1889–1977)** *English comedian, film actor, director and satirist*

Life is a tragedy when seen in close-up, but a comedy in long-shot.

In The Guardian, Obituary, 1977

Firbank, Ronald (1886–1926) *English novelist and short-story writer*

The world is disgracefully managed, one hardly knows to whom to complain. **Vainglory (1915)**

Gay, John (1685–1732) *English poet, dramatist and librettist*

Life is a jest; and all things show it.
I thought so once; but now I know it. **'My Own Epitaph' (1720)**

Hubbard, Elbert (1856–1915) *American author and editor*

Life is just one damned thing after another. **Philistine, 1909**

Lennon, John (1940–1980) *English rock musician*

Life is what happens to you when you're busy making other plans.
'Beautiful Boy', song, 1980

Lewis, Sir George Cornewall (1806–1863) *English statesman*

Life would be tolerable but for its amusements.
In Dictionary of National Biography

Maugham, William Somerset (1874–1965) *British writer*

Life is too short to do anything for oneself that one can pay others to do for one. **The Summing Up (1938)**

Nash, Ogden (1902–1971) *American humorous poet*

When I consider how my life is spent,
I hardly ever repent.
Hard Lines (1931), 'Reminiscent Reflection'

Santayana, George (1863–1952) *Spanish philosopher and poet*

There is no cure for birth and death save to enjoy the interval.
Soliloquies in England (1922)

Smith, Logan Pearsall (1865–1946) *American-born British writer*

People say that life is the thing, but I prefer reading.
Afterthoughts (1931)

Villiers de l'Isle-Adam, Philippe-Auguste (1838–1889)

French writer

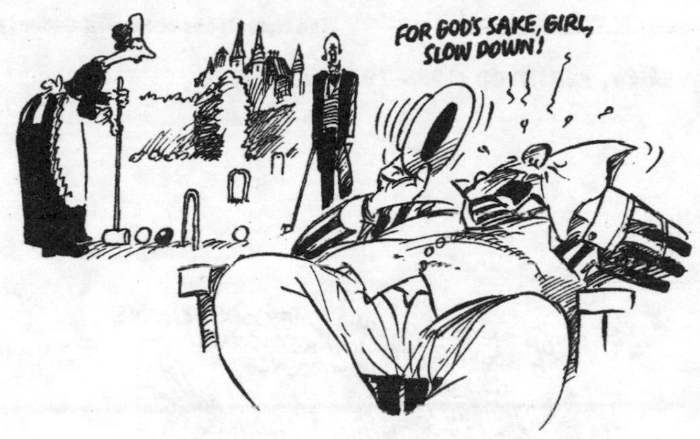
FOR GOD'S SAKE, GIRL,
SLOW DOWN!

Vivre? Les serviteurs feront cela pour nous. [Live? The servants will do that for us.] **Axel (1890)**

Wodehouse, P.G. (1881–1975) *English novelist*

I spent the afternoon musing on Life. If you come to think of it, what a queer thing Life is! So unlike anything else, don't you know, if you see what I mean. **My Man Jeeves (1919), 'Rallying Round Old George'**

LOVE

Balzac, Honoré de (1799–1850) *French novelist*

It is easier to be a lover than a husband, for the same reason that it is more difficult to show a ready wit all day long than to produce an occasional bon mot. **Attr.**

Bickerstaffe, Isaac **(c. 1733–c. 1808)** *Irish comic dramatist*

Perhaps it was right to dissemble your love,
But – why did you kick me downstairs? **'An Expostulation' (1789)**

Butler, Samuel **(1835–1902)** *English novelist, painter and philosopher*

'Tis better to have loved and lost than never to have lost at all.

The Way of All Flesh (1903)

God is Love, I dare say. But what a mischievous devil Love is.

The Note-Books of Samuel Butler (1912)

Chevalier, Maurice **(1888–1972)** *French actor*

ON THE OTHER HAND, ONE COULD CHOOSE A BOWLER HAT WITH REASONABLE CONFIDENCE!

Many a man has fallen in love with a girl in a light so dim he would not have chosen a suit by it. **Attr.**

Colman, the Elder, George **(1732–1794)** *English playwright*

Love and a cottage! Eh, Fanny! Ah, give me indifference and a coach and six! **The Clandestine Marriage (1766)**

Cope, Wendy **(1945–)** *English writer and poet*

2 cures for love

1. Don't see him. Don't phone or write a letter.
2. The easy way: get to know him better. **Attr.**

Fry, Christopher **(1907–)** *English dramatist*

Try thinking of love, or something.
Amor vincit insomnia. **A Sleep of Prisoners (1951)**

Graves, Robert **(1895–1985)** *English poet, novelist and critic*

In love as in sport, the amateur status must be strictly maintained.

Occupation: Writer

Hudson, Louise **(1958–)**

Now I go to films alone
watch a silent telephone
send myself a valentine
whisper softly 'I am mine'. **'Men, Who Needs Them'**

Jerrold, Douglas William **(1803–1857)** *English author and dramatist*

Love's like the measles – all the worse when it comes late in life.

Wit and Opinions of Douglas Jerrold (1859)

Lindsay, Norman **(1879–1969)** *Australian cartoonist*

The best love affairs are those we never had.

Bohemians of the Bulletin (1965)

Loos, Anita **(1893–1981)** *American humorous novelist and screenwriter*

Kissing your hand may make you feel very very good but a diamond and safire bracelet lasts forever. **Gentlemen Prefer Blondes (1925)**

Marx, Groucho **(1895–1977)** *American film comedian*

Send two dozen roses to Room 424 and put 'Emily, I love you' on the back of the bill. **A Night in Casablanca, film, 1945**

Perelman, S.J. **(1904–1979)** *American humorist, journalist and dramatist*

I tried to resist his overtures, but he plied me with symphonies, quartets, chamber music and cantatas.

Crazy Like a Fox (1944), 'The Love Decoy'

Shaw, George Bernard **(1856–1950)** *Irish dramatist and critic*

The fickleness of the women I love is only equalled by the infernal constancy of the women who love me. **The Philanderer (1898)**

Sterne, Laurence **(1713–1768)** *Irish-born English novelist*

Love, an' please your honour, is exactly like war, in this; that a soldier, though he has escaped three weeks complete o' Saturday night, – may nevertheless be shot through his heart on Sunday morning.

Tristram Shandy (1759–1767)

Symons, Michael Brooke **(1945–)** *Australian journalist and writer*

Love is what makes the world go around – that and clichés.

Sydney Morning Herald, 1970

Thackeray, William Makepeace **(1811–1863)** *English novelist*

Werther had a love for Charlotte
Such as words could never utter;
Would you know how first he met her?
She was cutting bread and butter.
Charlotte was a married lady,
And a moral man was Werther,
And for all the wealth of Indies,
Would do nothing for to hurt her.
So he sighed and pined and ogled,
And his passion boiled and bubbled,
Till he blew his silly brains out
And no more was by it troubled.
Charlotte, having seen his body
Borne before her on a shutter,
Like a well-conducted person,
Went on cutting bread and butter. **'Sorrows of Werther' (1855)**

CHARLOTTE'S FUNERAL CATERING
WE MAKE A GREAT TEAM, CHARLEY
BUTTER

MADNESS

Beckett, Samuel **(1906–1989)** *Irish author and playwright*

We are all born mad. Some remain so. **Waiting for Godot (1955)**

Beerbohm, Sir Max **(1872–1956)** *English writer and caricaturist*

Only the insane take themselves quite seriously. **Attr.**

Chesterton, G.K. **(1874–1936)** *English novelist, poet and critic*

The madman is not the man who has lost his reason. The madman is the man who has lost everything except his reason. **Orthodoxy (1908)**

Clare, John **(1793–1864)** *English poet*

Dear Sir, – I am in a Madhouse and quite forget your name or who you are. **Letter, 1860**

Dali, Salvador **(1904–1989)** *Spanish artist*

There is only one difference between a madman and me. I am not mad. **The American, 1956**

George II (1683–1760)

DECENT OF HIM TO ASK US
OVER FOR A BITE!
WOLFIE

Reply to the Duke of Newcastle who complained that General Wolfe was a madman
Mad, is he? Then I hope he will bite some of my other generals.

In Wilson, The Life and Letters of James Wolfe (1909)

Heller, Joseph (1923–) *American novelist*

Orr was crazy and could be grounded. All he had to do was ask; and as soon as he did, he would no longer be crazy and would have to fly more missions ... Yossarian was moved very deeply by the absolute simplicity of this clause of Catch-22 and let out a respectful whistle.

Catch-22 (1961)

Jung, Carl (1875–1961) *Swiss psychiatrist*

Show me a sane man and I will cure him for you. **The Observer, 1975**

Lee, Nathaniel (c. 1653–1692) *English dramatist*

Objecting to being confined in Bedlam
They called me mad, and I called them mad, and damn them, they outvoted me. **In Porter, A Social History of Madness**

Smollett, Tobias (1721–1771) *Scottish novelist*

I think for my part one half of the nation is mad – and the other not very sound. **The Adventures of Sir Launcelot Greaves (1762)**

Szasz, Thomas (1920–) *Hungarian-born American psychiatrist*

If you talk to God, you are praying; if God talks to you, you have schizophrenia. If the dead talk to you, you are a spiritualist; if God talks to you, you are a schizophrenic. **The Second Sin (1973)**

Voltaire (1694–1778) *French author and critic*

Men will always be mad and those who think they can cure them are the maddest of all. **Letter, 1762**

MANNERS

Coward, Sir Noël (1899–1973) *English dramatist, actor and composer*

Comedies of manners swiftly become obsolete when there are no longer any manners. **Relative Values (1951)**

Jarrell, Randall (1914–1965) *American poet, literary critic and translator*

To Americans English manners are far more frightening than none at all. **Pictures from an Institution (1954)**

Saki (Hector Hugh Munro) (1870–1916) *British journalist and writer*

I think she must have been very strictly brought up, she's so desperately anxious to do the wrong thing correctly. **Reginald (1904), 'Reginald on Worries'**

Theroux, Paul (1941–) *American novelist and travel writer*

The Japanese have perfected good manners and made them indistinguishable from rudeness. **The Great Railway Bazaar (1975)**

Twain, Mark (1835–1910) *American humorist and novelist*

Good breeding consists in concealing how much we think of ourselves and how little we think of other persons. **Notebooks (1935)**

MARRIAGE

Allen, Woody **(1935–)** *American film director, writer, actor and comedian*

It was partially my fault that we got divorced ... I tended to place my wife under a pedestal. **At a nightclub in Chicago, 1964**

Behan, Brendan **(1923–1964)** *Irish author*

I am married to Beatrice Salkeld, a painter. We have no children, except me. **Attr.**

Bennett, Alan **(1934–)** *English dramatist, actor and diarist*

On Sidney and Beatrice Webb
Two of the nicest people if ever there was one.
Forty Years On (1969) (not in the published script)

Bowra, Sir Maurice **(1898–1971)** *English classical scholar*

NICE OF MAURICE TO LEAVE HIS TEETH AS A WEDDING PRESENT!

On the wedding of a well-known literary couple in 1956
Splendid couple – slept with both of them. **Attr**

Braxfield, Lord **(1722–1799)** *Scottish 'hanging' judge*

To the butler who gave up his place because Lady Braxfield was always scolding him
Lord! Ye've little to complain o': ye may be thankfu' ye're no married to her. **In Cockburn, Memorials (1856)**

Butler, Samuel **(1835–1902)** *English novelist, painter and philosopher*

Marriage is distinctly and repeatedly excluded from heaven. Is this because it is thought likely to mar the general felicity?
Samuel Butler's Notebooks (1951)

It was very good of God to let Carlyle and Mrs Carlyle marry one another and so make only two people miserable instead of four, besides being very amusing. **Letter to Miss Savage, 1884**

Eastwood, Clint **(1930–)** *American film actor and director*

There's only one way to have a happy marriage and as soon as I learn what it is I'll get married again. **Attr.**

Gabor, Zsa-Zsa **(1919–)** *Hungarian film actress*

Husbands are like fires. They go out when unattended. **Newsweek, 1960**

A man in love is incomplete until he has married. Then he's finished.
Newsweek, 1960

Her answer to the question 'How many husbands have you had?'
You mean apart from my own? **Attr.**

Gay, John **(1685–1732)** *English poet, dramatist and librettist*

One wife is too much for most husbands to hear,
But two at a time there's no mortal can bear.
This way, and that way, and which way I will,
What would comfort the one, t'other wife would take ill.
The Beggar's Opera (1728), III.xi

Marx, Groucho **(1895–1977)** *American film comedian*

My husband is dead.
– I'll bet he's just using that as an excuse.
I was with him to the end.
– No wonder he passed away.
I held him in my arms and kissed him.
– So it was murder! **Duck Soup, film, 1933**

Muir, Frank **(1920–1998)** *English writer, humorist and broadcaster*

It has been said that a bride's attitude towards her betrothed can be summed up in three words: Aisle. Altar. Hymn.

Upon My Word!, 'A Jug of Wine', with Dennis Norden

Parker, Dorothy **(1893–1967)** *American poet, writer, critic and wit*

Said of her husband on the day their divorce became final

Oh, don't worry about Alan ... Alan will always land on somebody's feet.

In J. Keats, You Might As Well Live (1970)

Peacock, Thomas Love **(1785–1866)** *English novelist and poet*

Sir, I have quarrelled with my wife; and a man who has quarrelled with his wife is absolved from all duty to his country.

Nightmare Abbey (1818)

Punch *British humorous periodical, founded 1841*

Advice to persons about to marry – 'Don't!' **1845**

Bishop: Who is it that sees and hears all we do, and before whom even I am but as a crushed worm?

Page: The Missus, my Lord. **1880**

Richelieu, Duc de **(1766–1822)** *French courtier, soldier and statesman*

On discovering his wife with her lover

Madame, you must really be more careful. Suppose it had been someone else who found you like this.

In D. Wallechinsky, The Book of Lists (1977)

Rowland, Helen **(1875–1950)** *American writer*

When you see what some girls marry, you realize how they must hate to work for a living. **Reflections of a Bachelor Girl (1909)**

Before marriage, a man will lie awake thinking about something you said; after marriage, he'll fall asleep before you finish saying it.

In Cowan, The Wit of Women

Russell, Lord John **(1792–1878)** *English statesman and writer*

When asked to describe a suitable punishment for bigamy

Two mothers-in-law. **Attr.**

Saki (Hector Hugh Munro) **(1870–1916)** *British journalist and writer*

The Western custom of one wife and hardly any mistresses.

Reginald in Russia (1910), 'A Young Turkish Catastrophe'

Spring-Rice, Cecil Arthur **(1859–1918)** *English diplomat*

I am the Dean, and this is Mrs Liddell;
She the first, and I the second fiddle.

Unofficially altered first couplet of 'The Masque of Balliol'

Thatcher, Denis **(1915–)** *English businessman; husband of Margaret Thatcher*

Replying to the question 'Who wears the pants in this house?'
I do, and I also wash and iron them. **The Times (Los Angeles), 1981**

Thomas, Irene **(1920–)** *English writer and broadcaster*

It should be a very happy marriage – they are both so much in love with him. **Attr.**

Ward, Artemus **(1834–1867)** *American humorist; journalist, editor and lecturer*

If you mean gettin hitched, I'M IN!

Artemus Ward, His Book (1862), 'The Showman's Courtship'

He is dreadfully married. He's the most married man I ever saw in my life. **Artemus Ward's Lecture (1869), 'Brigham Young's Palace'**

Wilde, Oscar **(1854–1900)** *Irish dramatist, novelist, critic and wit*

The amount of women in London who flirt with their own husbands is perfectly scandalous. It looks so bad. It is simply washing one's clean linen in public. **The Importance of Being Earnest (1895)**

You don't seem to realise, that in married life three is company and two is none. **The Importance of Being Earnest (1895)**

I am not in favour of long engagements. They give people the opportunity of finding out each other's character before marriage, which I think is never advisable. **The Importance of Being Earnest (1895)**

Wodehouse, P.G. **(1881–1975)** *English novelist*

All the unhappy marriages come from the husbands having brains. What good are brains to a man? They only unsettle him.

The Adventures of Sally

Like so many substantial Americans, he had married young and kept on marrying, springing from blonde to blonde like the chamois of the Alps leaping from crag to crag.

In R. Usborne, Wodehouse at Work to the End (1976)

MEDICINE

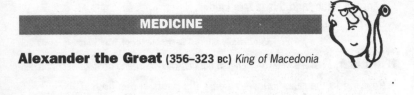

Alexander the Great **(356–323 BC)** *King of Macedonia*

I am dying with the help of too many physicians. **Attr**

Anonymous

We've made great medical progress in the last generation. What used to be merely an itch is now an allergy.

Asquith, Margot **(1864–1945)** *Scottish political hostess and writer*

The King told me he would never have died if it had not been for that fool Dawson of Penn. **In K. Rose, King George V (1983)**

Goldwyn, Samuel **(1882–1974)** *Polish-born American film producer*

Any man who goes to a psychiatrist should have his head examined.

In Zierold, Moguls (1969)

Loos, Anita **(1893–1981)** *American humorous novelist and screenwriter*

So then Dr Froyd said that all I needed was to cultivate a few inhibitions and get some sleep. **Gentlemen Prefer Blondes (1925)**

Muir, Frank **(1920–1998)** *English writer, humorist and broadcaster*

I've examined your son's head, Mr Glum, and there's nothing there.

Take It from Here, BBC radio programme, 1957, with Dennis Norden

Punch *British humorous periodical, founded 1841*

What sort of a doctor is he?
Oh, well, I don't know very much about his ability; but he's got a very good bedside manner! **1884**

Satie, Erik **(1866–1925)** *French experimental composer*

Mon médecin m'a toujours dit de fumer. Il ajoute à ses conseils: 'Fumez, mon ami: sans cela, un autre fumera à votre place.' [My doctor has always told me to smoke. He explains himself thus: 'Smoke, my friend. If you don't, someone else will smoke in your place.']

Mémoires d'un amnésique (1924)

Stockwood, Mervyn **(1913–)** *English Anglican prelate*

A psychiatrist is a man who goes to the Folies-Bergère and looks at the audience. **The Observer, 1961**

Wall, Max **(1908–1990)** *English comedian, stage actor and radio performer*

To me Adler will always be Jung. **Telegram to Larry Adler on his 60th birthday**

Williams, Tennessee **(1911–1983)** *American dramatist, novelist and short-story writer*

Explaining why he had stopped seeing his psychoanalyst
He was meddling too much in my private life. **Attr.**

Wodehouse, P.G. **(1881–1975)** *English novelist*

His ideas of first-aid stopped short at squirting soda-water.
My Man Jeeves (1919), 'Doing Clarence a Bit of Good'

MEMORY

Fenton, James **(1949–)** *British poet, journalist and critic*

How comforting it is, once or twice a year
To get together and forget the old times.
The Memory of War. Poems 1968–1982 (1983), 'A German Requiem'

Marx, Groucho **(1895–1977)** *American film comedian*

I never forget a face, but I'll make an exception in your case.
The Guardian, 1965

Spooner, William **(1844–1930)** *English clergyman and university warden*

I remember your name perfectly, but I just can't think of your face. **Attr.**

Svevo, Italo **(1861–1928)** *Italian novelist*

There are three things I always forget. Names, faces and – the third I can't remember. **Attr.**

MEN

Anonymous

Whilst Adam slept, Eve from his side arose:
Strange his first sleep should be his last repose. **'The Consequence'**

Bombeck, Erma **(1927–1996)**

What's wrong with you men? Would hair stop growing on your chest if you asked directions somewhere?

When You Look Like Your Passport Photo, It's Time to Go Home (1991)

Cope, Wendy **(1945–)** *English writer and poet*

There are so many kinds of awful men –
One can't avoid them all. She often said
She'd never make the same mistake again:
She always made a new mistake instead.

Making Cocoa for Kingsley Amis (1986), 'Rondeau Redoublé'

Bloody Christmas, here again,
Let us raise a loving cup:
Peace on earth, goodwill to men,
And make them do the washing-up. **'Another Christmas Poem'**

Gabor, Zsa-Zsa **(1919–)** *Hungarian film actress*

Never despise what it says in the women's magazines: it may not be subtle but neither are men. **The Observer, 1976**

Hill, Reginald **(1936–)** *English author and playwright*

He created a man who was hard of head, blunt of speech, knew which side his bread was buttered on, and above all took no notice of women. Then God sent him forth to multiply in Yorkshire.

Pictures of Perfection (1994)

Keillor, Garrison (1942–) *American writer*

Years ago, manhood was an opportunity for achievement, and now it is a problem to be overcome. **The Book of Guys (1994)**

Lerner, Alan Jay (1918–1986) *American lyricist and screenwriter*

Why can't a woman be more like a man?
Men are so honest, so thoroughly square;
Eternally noble, historically fair. **My Fair Lady (1956)**

Mencken, H.L. (1880–1956) *American journalist and linguist*

Men have a much better time of it than women. For one thing, they marry later. For another thing, they die earlier.

A Mencken Chrestomathy (1949)

Rowland, Helen (1875–1950) *American writer*

Never trust a husband too far, nor a bachelor too near.

The Rubaiyat of a Bachelor (1925)

Sévigné, Mme de (1626–1696) *French letter writer*

The more I see of men, the more I admire dogs. **Attr**

Twain, Mark **(1835–1910)** *American humorist and novelist*

Responding to the question 'In a world without women what would men become?'

Scarce, sir. Mighty scarce. **Attr.**

West, Mae **(1892–1980)** *American actress and scriptwriter*

A man in the house is worth two in the street.

Belle of the Nineties, film, 1934

When women go wrong, men go right after them.

In J. Weintraub (ed.), The Wit and Wisdom of Mae West (1967)

Woddis, Roger **(1917–1993)** *British satirical poet and scriptwriter*

Men play the game; women know the score. **The Observer, 1982**

MISTAKES

Destouches, Philippe Néricault **(1680–1754)**

Les absents ont toujours tort. [The absent are always in the wrong.]

L'Obstacle Imprévu (1717)

Johnson, Samuel **(1709–1784)** *English lexicographer, poet and critic*

Asked the reason for a mistake in his Dictionary

Ignorance, madam, sheer ignorance.

In Boswell, The Life of Samuel Johnson (1791)

Reagan, Ronald **(1911–)** *Politician and film actor; US President 1981–89*

You know, by the time you reach my age, you've made plenty of mistakes if you've lived your life properly. **The Observer, 1987**

Thurber, James **(1894–1961)** *American humorist, writer and illustrator*

Well, if I called the wrong number, why did you answer the phone?

Cartoon caption in The New Yorker, 1937

MONEY

Baring, Maurice **(1874–1945)** *English poet, novelist and journalist*

If you would know what the Lord God thinks of money, you have only to look at those to whom He gives it. **Attr.**

Barzan, Gerald

Mother always said that honesty was the best policy, and money isn't everything. She was wrong about other things too. **Attr.**

Belloc, Hilaire **(1870–1953)** *French-born English writer and poet*

Lord Finchley tried to mend the Electric Light
Himself. It struck him dead: And serve him right!
It is the business of the wealthy man
To give employment to the artisan. **More Peers (1911), 'Lord Finchley'**

I'm tired of Love: I'm still more tired of Rhyme.
But Money gives me pleasure all the time. **'Fatigue' (1923)**

Benchley, Robert **(1889–1945)** *American humorist and actor*

Comment on being told his request for a loan had been granted

I don't trust a bank that would lend money to such a poor risk. **Attr.**

Huxley, Sir Julian **(1887–1975)** *English biologist and humanist*

We all know how the size of sums of money appears to vary in a remarkable way according as they are being paid in or paid out.

Essays of a Biologist

Johnson, Samuel **(1709–1784)** *English lexicographer, poet and critic*

You never find people labouring to convince you that you may live very happily upon a plentiful fortune.

In Boswell, The Life of Samuel Johnson (1791)

There are few ways in which a man can be more innocently employed than in getting money. **In Boswell, The Life of Samuel Johnson (1791)**

Marx, Groucho **(1895–1977)** *American film comedian*

What's a thousand dollars? Mere chicken feed. A poultry matter.

Animal Crackers, film, 1930

Milligan, Spike **(1918–)** *English humorist*

Money can't buy friends, but you can get a better class of enemy.

Puckoon (1963)

Saki (Hector Hugh Munro) **(1870–1916)** *British journalist and writer*

All decent people live beyond their incomes nowadays, and those who aren't respectable live beyond other people's. A few gifted individuals manage to do both. **The Chronicles of Clovis (1911), 'The Match-Maker'**

Sheridan, Tom **(1775–1817)** *English colonial administrator and poet*

To his father, after learning that he was to be cut out of his will with a shilling

I'm sorry to hear that, sir, you don't happen to have the shilling about you now, do you? **In L. Harris, The Fine Art of Political Wit (1965)**

Sickert, Walter **(1860–1942)** *British artist*

Nothing knits man to man … like the frequent passage from hand to hand of cash. **'The Language of Art'**

Tucker, Sophie **(1884–1966)** *Russian-born American vaudeville singer*

I've been poor and I've been rich. Rich is better.

In Cowan, The Wit of Women

Twain, Mark **(1835–1910)** *American humorist and novelist*

Agreeing with a friend's comment that the money of a particular rich industrialist was 'tainted'

That's right. 'Taint yours, and 'taint mine. **Attr.**

A banker is a person who lends you his umbrella when the sun is shining and wants it back the minute it rains. **Attr.**

MUSIC

Ade, George (1866–1944) *American fabulist and playwright*

The music teacher came twice a week to bridge the awful gap between Dorothy and Chopin. **Attr.**

Appleton, Sir Edward Victor (1892–1965) *English physicist*

HE'S OUT THERE SO WE'RE DOING IT IN SIGN LANGUAGE!
PUCCINI'S

I do not mind what language an opera is sung in so long as it is a language I don't understand. **The Observer, 'Sayings of the Week', 1955**

Beecham, Sir Thomas **(1879–1961)** *English conductor and impresario*

The sound of the harpsichord resembles that of a bird-cage played with toasting-forks. **Attr.**

Of Bruckner's 7th Symphony

In the first movement alone, I took note of six pregnancies and at least four miscarriages. **Attr.**

Morton, J.B. ('Beachcomber') **(1893–1979)** *English journalist, humorist and author*

Wagner is the Puccini of music.

In Rupert Hart-Davis, Lyttelton Hart-Davis Letters

Newman, Ernest **(1868–1959)** *English music critic and writer*

I sometimes wonder which would be nicer – an opera without an interval, or an interval without an opera.

In Peter Heyworth (ed.), Berlioz, Romantic and Classic

Randolph, David

On Parsifal

The kind of opera that starts at six o'clock and after it has been going three hours, you look at your watch and it says 6.20.

In The Frank Muir Book: An Irreverant Companion to Social History (1976)

Rossini, Gioacchino (1792–1868) *Italian composer*

Monsieur Wagner a de beaux moments, mais de mauvais quart d'heures. [Wagner has beautiful moments but awful quarters of an hour.]

In E. Naumann, Italienische Tondichter (1883)

Sarasate (y Navascués), Pablo (1844–1908) *Spanish violinist and composer*

On being hailed as a genius by a critic

A genius! For thirty-seven years I've practised fourteen hours a day, and now they call me a genius! **Attr.**

Sargent, Sir Malcolm (1895–1967) *English conductor*

Rehearsing a female chorus in 'For Unto Us a Child is Born' from Handel's Messiah

Just a little more reverence, please, and not so much astonishment.

Attr.

Satie, Erik (1866–1925) *French experimental composer*

NOTHING TO IT, MATE. STICK IT UNDER YOUR CHIN!

Direction on one of his piano pieces

To be played with both hands in the pocket. **Attr.**

Schnabel, Artur **(1882–1951)** *Austrian pianist and composer*

Advice given to the pianist Vladimir Horowitz

When a piece gets difficult make faces. **Attr.**

Schoenberg, Arnold **(1874–1951)** *Austrian composer*

When told that his violin concerto would need a soloist with six fingers

Very well, I can wait. **Attr.**

Slezak, Leo **(1873–1946)** *Austrian-born American tenor*

When the mechanical swan left the stage without him during a performance of Lohengrin

What time is the next swan? **In W. Slezak, What Time's the Next Swan? (1962)**

Thomas, Irene **(1920–)** *English writer and broadcaster*

The cello is not one of my favourite instruments. It has such a lugubrious sound, like someone reading a will. **Attr.**

Toscanini, Arturo **(1867–1957)** *Italian conductor*

Rebuking an incompetent orchestra
After I die, I shall return to earth as a gatekeeper of a bordello and I won't let any of you – not a one of you – enter!

In Howard Taubman, The Maestro: The Life of Arturo Toscanini (1951)

Criticizing the playing of an Austrian orchestra during rehearsal
Can't you read? The score demands *con amore*, and what are you doing? You are playing it like married men! **Attr.**

Rebuking an incompetent woman cellist
Madame, there you sit with that magnificent instrument between your legs, and all you can do is scratch it! **Attr.**

Twain, Mark (1835–1910) *American humorist and novelist*

I have been told that Wagner's music is better than it sounds.
Autobiography (1959 edition)

Wharton, Edith (1862–1937) *American writer*

An unalterable and unquestioned law of the musical world required that the German text of French operas sung by Swedish artists should be translated into Italian for the clearer understanding of English speaking audiences. **The Age of Innocence (1920)**

NEWS

Arnold, Harry *British journalist*

Commenting on the news that the Queen had started to refer privately to Royal reporters as 'scum'
At least we're la crème de la scum. **The Observer, 1995**

Balfour, A. J. (1848–1930) *Scottish statesman*

Frank Harris ... said ...: 'The fact is, Mr Balfour, all the faults of the age come from Christianity and journalism.' To which Arthur replied ... 'Christianity, of course ... but why journalism?'
In Margot Asquith, Autobiography (1920)

Bevan, Aneurin (1897–1960) *Welsh Labour politician*

I read the newspapers avidly. It is my one form of continuous fiction.
The Observer, 1960

Bradbury, Malcolm (1932–) *English novelist, critic and academic*

Reading someone else's newspaper is like sleeping with someone else's wife. Nothing seems to be precisely in the right place, and when you find what you are looking for, it is not clear then how to respond to it.

Stepping Westward (1965)

Eldershaw, M. Barnard (1897–1987) *Australian writer*

Journalists are people who take in one another's washing and then sell it. **Plaque with Laurel (1937)**

Murray, David (1888–1962) *British journalist*

A reporter is a man who has renounced everything in life but the world, the flesh, and the devil. **The Observer, 1931**

Sheridan, Richard Brinsley (1751–1816) *Irish comic dramatist*

The newspapers! Sir, they are the most villainous – licentious –

abominable – infernal – Not that I ever read them – No – I make it a rule never to look into a newspaper. **The Critic (1779)**

Stevenson, Adlai **(1900–1965)** *American lawyer and statesman*

An editor is one who separates the wheat from the chaff and prints the chaff. **In Bill Adler, The Stevenson Wit (1966)**

Swaffer, Hannen **(1879–1962)**

Freedom of the press in Britain is freedom to print such of the proprietor's prejudices as the advertisers don't object to.

In Driberg, Swaff (1974)

Wilde, Oscar **(1854–1900)** *Irish dramatist, novelist, critic and wit*

There is much to be said in favour of modern journalism. By giving us the opinions of the uneducated, it keeps us in touch with the ignorance of the community. **'The Critic as Artist' (1891)**

Wolfe, Humbert **(1886–1940)** *English poet and critic*

You cannot hope
To bribe or twist,
thank God! the
British journalist.
But, seeing what
the man will do
unbribed, there's
no occasion to. **'Over the Fire' (1930)**

PEACE

Belloc, Hilaire **(1870–1953)** *French-born English writer and poet*

Pale Ebenezer thought it wrong to fight,
But Roaring Bill (who killed him) thought it right.

Sonnets and Verse (second ed. 1938), 'The Pacifist'

Bierce, Ambrose **(1842–c. 1914)** *American writer, journalist and soldier*

Peace: In international affairs, a period of cheating between two periods of fighting. **The Cynic's Word Book (1906)**

Holmes, Oliver Wendell **(1809–1894)** *American physician and writer*

Wisdom has taught us to be calm and meek,
To take one blow, and turn the other cheek;
It is not written what a man shall do
If the rude caitiff smite the other too! **'Non-Resistance' (1861)**

Mayhew, Christopher **(1915–1997)**

On the Munich Agreement

The peace that passeth all understanding. **Speech, 1938**

PHILOSOPHY

Bowen, Lord **(1835–1894)** *English judge and translator of Virgil*

On a metaphysician: A blind man in a dark room – looking for a black hat – which isn't there. **Attr.**

Chamfort, Nicolas **(1741–1794)** *French writer*

Je dirais volontiers des métaphysiciens ce que Scalinger disait des Basques, on dit qu'ils s'entendent, mais je n'en crois rien. [I am tempted to say about metaphysicians what Scalinger would say about the Basques: they are said to understand one another, but I don't believe a word of it.] **Maximes et Pensées (1796)**

Edwards, Oliver **(1711–1791)**

I have tried too in my time to be a philosopher; but, I don't know how, cheerfulness was always breaking in.

In Boswell, The Life of Samuel Johnson (1791)

Russell, Bertrand **(1872–1970)** *Welsh philosopher, mathematician and author*

Organic life, we are told, has developed gradually from the protozoon to the philosopher, and this development, we are assured, is indubitably an advance. Unfortunately it is the philosopher, not the protozoon, who gives us this assurance. **Mysticism and Logic (1918)**

PLAGIARISM

Bierce, Ambrose (1842–c. 1914) *American writer, journalist and soldier*

Plagiarize: To take the thought or style of another writer whom one has never, never read. **The Enlarged Devil's Dictionary (1961)**

Mizner, Wilson (1876–1933)

When you steal from one author, it's plagiarism; if you steal from many, it's research. **Attr.**

Sheridan, Richard Brinsley (1751–1816) *Irish comic dramatist*

All that can be said is, that two people happened to hit on the same thought – and Shakespeare made use of it first, that's all. **The Critic (1779)**

Sullivan, Sir Arthur (1842–1900) *English composer*

Accused of plagiarism
We all have the same eight notes to work with. **Attr.**

Whistler, James McNeill (1834–1903) *American painter and etcher*

Oscar Wilde: I wish I had said that.
Whistler: You will, Oscar, you will. **In Ingleby, Oscar Wilde (1907)**

PLEASURE

Bierce, Ambrose (1842–c. 1914) *American writer, journalist and soldier*

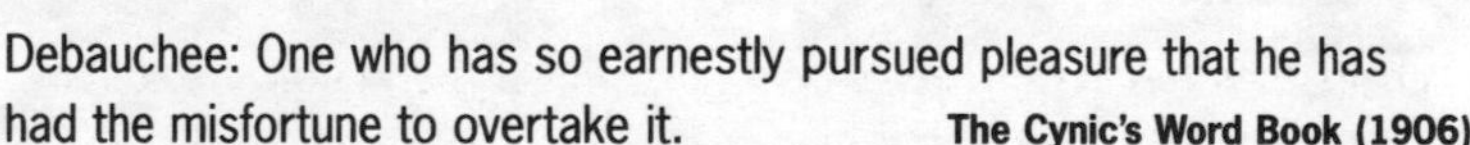

Debauchee: One who has so earnestly pursued pleasure that he has had the misfortune to overtake it. **The Cynic's Word Book (1906)**

Lamb, Charles (1775–1834) *English essayist*

The greatest pleasure I know, is to do a good action by stealth, and to have it found out by accident. **'Table Talk by the Late Elia'**

O'Rourke, P.J. (1947–) *American writer and humorist*

After all, what is your hosts' purpose in having a party? Surely not for you to enjoy yourself; if that were their sole purpose, they'd have simply sent champagne and women over to your place by taxi. **Attr.**

Thomas, Gwyn **(1913–1981)** *Welsh novelist, dramatist and teacher*

WORST OUTBREAK OF THE DEADLY
BLACK HILARITY SINCE...

There are still parts of Wales where the only concession to gaiety is a striped shroud. **Punch, 1958**

Woollcott, Alexander **(1887–1943)** *American journalist and critic*

All the things I really like to do are either immoral, illegal, or fattening.

In R.E. Drennan, Wit's End (1973)

POETRY

Auden, W.H. **(1907–1973)** *English poet*

A poet's hope: to be,
like some valley cheese,
local, but prized elsewhere. **'Shorts II'**

Beer, Thomas **(1889–1940)**

I agree with one of your reputable critics that a taste for drawing-rooms has spoiled more poets than ever did a taste for gutters.

The Mauve Decade (1926)

Cope, Wendy **(1945–)** *English writer and poet*

I used to think all poets were Byronic –
Mad, bad and dangerous to know.
And then I met a few. Yes it's ironic –
I used to think all poets were Byronic.
They're mostly wicked as a ginless tonic
And wild as pension plans. Not long ago
I used to think all poets were Byronic –
Mad, bad and dangerous to know.

Making Cocoa for Kingsley Amis (1986), 'Triolet'

Ewart, Gavin **(1916–1995)** *English poet*

Good light verse is better than bad heavy verse any day of the week.

Penultimate Poems (1989)

James VI of Scotland and I of England **(1566–1625)**

Dr Donne's verses are like the peace of God; they pass all understanding. **Attr.**

Jarrell, Randall **(1914–1965)** *American poet and critic*

Some poetry seems to have been written on typewriters by other typewriters. **Attr.**

Klopstock, Friedrich **(1724–1803)** *German religious and lyric poet*

Of one of his poems

God and I both knew what it meant once; now God alone knows. **Attr.**

Porson, Richard **(1759–1808)** *English scholar of Greek*

Giving his opinion of the poems of Robert Southey

Your works will be read after Shakespeare and Milton are forgotten – and not till then. **In L. Meissen, Quotable Anecdotes**

Preston, Keith **(1884–1927)** *American poet, columnist and teacher*

Of all the literary scenes
Saddest this sight to me:
The graves of little magazines
Who died to make verse free. **'The Liberators'**

POLITICS AND POLITICIANS

Adams, Douglas **(1952–)** *English author and scriptwriter*

Anyone who is capable of getting themselves made President should on no account be allowed to do the job.

The Hitch Hiker's Guide to the Galaxy (1979)

Allen, Dave **(1936–)** *Irish comedian and TV personality*

If John Major was drowning, his whole life would pass in front of him and he wouldn't be in it. **On stage, 1991, quoted in The Independent, 1993**

Anonymous

Don't tell my mother I'm in politics – she thinks I play the piano in a whorehouse. **American saying from the Depression**

Asquith, Herbert **(1852–1928)** *English Liberal statesman, politician and Prime Minister*

On Bonar Law

It is fitting that we should have buried the Unknown Prime Minister by the side of the Unknown Soldier.

Remark supposedly made at Bonar Law's funeral, November 1923

On the reason for the three sets of figures kept by the War Office
One to mislead the public; another to mislead the Cabinet, and the third to mislead itself. **In Alastair Horne, The Price of Glory (1962)**

Baldwin, Stanley (1867–1947) *English statesman*

On becoming Prime Minister
I met Curzon in Downing Street, from whom I got the sort of greeting a corpse would give to an undertaker. **Remark, 1933**

Beaverbrook, Lord (1879–1964) *British newspaper proprietor and politician*

Of Lloyd George
He did not care in which direction the car was travelling, so long as he remained in the driver's seat. **New Statesman, 1963**

Bevan, Aneurin (1897–1960) *Welsh Labour politician*

Listening to a speech by Chamberlain is like paying a visit to Woolworths; everything in its place and nothing over sixpence.
In Tribune, 1937

Bevin, Ernest (1881-1951) *English trade unionist and Labour politician*

When told that another Labourite was 'his own worst enemy'
Not while I'm alive, he ain't. **In M. Foot, Aneurin Bevan 1945–60 (1975)**

Bright, John (1811–1889) *English statesman and social reformer*

This party of two is like the Scotch terrier that was so covered with hair that you could not tell which was the head and which was the tail.
Speech, House of Commons, 1866

Of Disraeli
He is a self-made man, and worships his creator. **Remark, c.1868**

Brown, George (1914–1985) *British statesman and Labour Party leader*

Most British statesmen have either drunk too much or womanized too much. I never fell into the second category. **The Observer, 1974**

Clemenceau, Georges (1841–1929) *French statesman*

Mr Wilson bores me with his Fourteen Points; why, God Almighty has only ten. **In Wintle and Kenin, Dictionary of Biographical Quotations**

Cook, Peter (1937–1995) *English comic writer and comedian*

Giving an impersonation of Harold Macmillan
We exchanged many frank words in our respective languages.
Beyond the Fringe,1961

Devonshire, Duke of (1833–1908) *English statesman and Liberal politician*

I dreamt that I was making a speech in the House. I woke up, and by Jove I was! **In W.S. Churchill, Thought and Adventures**

Fields, W.C. (1880–1946) *American comic film actor*

Hell, I never vote for anybody. I always vote against.
In Robert Lewis Taylor, W. C. Fields: His Follies and Fortunes (1950)

Hale, Edward Everett (1822–1909) *American preacher and writer*

'Do you pray for the senators, Dr Hale?' 'No, I look at the senators and I pray for the country.' **In Van Wyck Brooks, New England Indian Summer (1940)**

Jarrell, Randall (1914–1965) *American poet and critic*

President Robbins was so well adjusted to his environment that sometimes you could not tell which was the environment and which was President Robbins. **Pictures from an Institution (1954)**

Lloyd George, David (1863–1945) *Welsh Liberal statesman*

When they circumcised Herbert Samuel they threw away the wrong bit.
Attr. in The Listener, 1978

Longworth, Alice Roosevelt (1884–1980) *American author, hostess and wit*

Of John Calvin Coolidge, US President 1923–1929
He looks as if he had been weaned on a pickle. **Crowded Hours (1933)**

Maudling, Reginald (1917–1977) *English politician*

Remark made on being replaced in the Shadow Cabinet by John Davies, his elder by four years
There comes a time in every man's life when he must make way for an older man. **The Guardian, 1976**

Milligan, Spike (1918–) *English humorist*

Remark made about a pre-election poll
One day the don't-knows will get in, and then where will we be? **Attr.**

Reagan, Ronald **(1911–)** *Politician and film actor; US President 1981–89*

Politics is supposed to be the second oldest profession. I have come to understand that it bears a very close resemblance to the first.

Remark at a conference, 1977

On his challenger, Walter Mondale, in the 1984 election campaign
I will not make age an issue of this campaign. I am not going to exploit for political purposes my opponent's youth and inexperience.

TV debate, 1984

To the surgeons about to operate on him after he was wounded in an assassination attempt
Please assure me that you are all Republicans!

In P. Boller, Presidential Anecdotes (1981)

Sahl, Mort **(1927–)** *American comedian*

Washington could not tell a lie; Nixon could not tell the truth; Reagan cannot tell the difference. **The Observer, 1987**

Sheridan, Richard Brinsley **(1751–1816)** *Irish comic dramatist*

Reply to Mr Dundas
The Right Honourable Gentleman is indebted to his memory for his jests, and to his imagination for his facts.

Speech, House of Commons, in Moore, Memoirs of the Life of Sheridan (1825), 21

Smith, F.E. **(1872–1930)** *English lawyer and statesman*

Winston [Churchill] has devoted the best years of his life to preparing his impromptu speeches. **Attr.**

Stevenson, Adlai **(1900–1965)** *American lawyer and statesman*

A politician is a statesman who approaches every question with an open mouth. **In L. Harris, The Fine Art of Political Wit**

Thomas, Norman M. **(1884–1968)** *American socialist, editor and writer*

Referring to his lack of success in presidential campaigns
While I'd rather be right than president, at any time I'm ready to be both.

In A. Whitman, Come to Judgment

Thorpe, Jeremy **(1929–)** *English Liberal politician*

Remark on Macmillan's Cabinet purge, 1962
Greater love hath no man than this, that he lay down his friends for his life. **Speech, House of Commons, 1962**

Truman, Harry S. **(1884–1972)** *US President 1945–53*

Referring to Vice-President Nixon's nomination for President
You don't set a fox to watching the chickens just because he has a lot of experience in the hen house. **Speech, 1960**

A statesman is a politician who's been dead ten or fifteen years. **Attr.**

Twain, Mark **(1835–1910)** *American humorist and novelist*

The radical invents the views. When he has worn them out, the conservative adopts them. **Notebooks (1935)**

Ustinov, Sir Peter **(1921–)** *English actor, dramatist, writer and wit*

When Mrs Thatcher says she has a nostalgia for Victorian values I don't think she realises that 90 per cent of her nostalgia would be satisfied in the Soviet Union. **The Observer, 1987**

Valéry, Paul **(1871–1945)** *French poet and writer*

La politique est l'art d'empêcher les gens de se mêler de ce qui les regarde. [Politics is the art of preventing people from becoming involved in affairs which concern them.] **Tel quel 2 (As Such 2, 1943)**

Vidal, Gore **(1925–)** *American novelist, dramatist, essayist, critic and poet*

There's a lot to be said for being nouveau riche and the Reagans mean to say it all. **The Observer, 1981**

Wallace, Edgar **(1875–1932)** *English novelist, dramatist and journalist*

Said when a candidate for Parliament

A writer of crook stories ought never to stop seeking new material.

In Alan Hodge, The Long Weekend (1940)

Waugh, Evelyn **(1903–1966)** *English journalist and novelist*

He stood twice for Parliament, but so diffidently that his candidature passed almost unnoticed. **Decline and Fall (1928)**

She had heard someone say something about an Independent Labour Party, and was furious that she had not been asked.

Vile Bodies (1930)

Pappenhacker says that every time you are polite to a proletarian you are helping to bolster up the capitalist system. **Scoop (1938)**

Whitehorn, Katherine (1926–) *English journalist and writer*

It is a pity, as my husband says, that more politicians are not bastards by birth instead of vocation. **The Observer, 1964**

Whitelaw, William (1918–) *English politician and landowner*

I am not prepared to go about the country stirring up apathy. **Attr.**

Wilson, Harold (1916–1995) *English Labour politician*

Of Tony Benn

He immatures with age. **Attr., BBC programme, 1995**

POVERTY

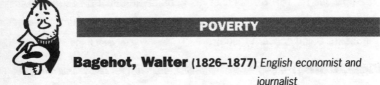

Bagehot, Walter (1826–1877) *English economist and journalist*

Poverty is an anomaly to rich people. It is very difficult to make out why people who want dinner do not ring the bell. **Literary Studies (1879)**

Cowper, William (1731–1800) *English poet*

Of a burglar

He found it inconvenient to be poor. **'Charity' (1782)**

Marx, Groucho (1895–1977) *American film comedian*

Look at me: I worked my way up from nothing to a state of extreme poverty. **Monkey Business, film, 1931**

Peacock, Thomas Love (1785–1866) *English novelist and poet*

Respectable means rich, and decent means poor. I should die if I heard my family called decent. **Crotchet Castle (1831)**

Shuter, Edward (1728–1776) *English comic actor*

Explaining why he did not mend the holes in his stocking

A hole is the accident of a day, but a darn is premeditated poverty. **Dictionary of National Biography (1897)**

Tracy, Spencer **(1900–1967)** *American film actor*

Of leaner times in his life
There were times my pants were so thin I could sit on a dime and tell if it was heads or tails. **In L. Swindell, Spencer Tracy**

PRAISE

Bierce, Ambrose **(1842–c. 1914)** *American writer, journalist and soldier*

Eulogy: Praise of a person who has either the advantages of wealth and power, or the consideration to be dead.

The Enlarged Devil's Dictionary (1961)

Proverb

Self-praise is no recommendation.

Tree, Sir Herbert Beerbohm **(1853–1917)** *English actor-manager*

The only man who wasn't spoilt by being lionized was Daniel.

In Hesketh Pearson, Beerbohm Tree (1956)

Voltaire **(1694–1778)** *French author and critic*

Giving a funeral oration
He was a great patriot, a humanitarian, a loyal friend – provided, of course, that he really is dead. **Attr.**

PRISON

Bottomley, Horatio William **(1860–1933)** *English journalist, financier and politician*

When spotted sewing mailbags during his imprisonment for misappropriation of funds
Visitor: Ah, Bottomley, sewing?
Bottomley: No, reaping. **Attr.**

Ingrams, Richard **(1937–)** *British journalist*

On the prospect of going to jail, 1976
The only thing I really mind about going to prison is the thought of Lord Longford coming to visit me. **Attr.**

Waugh, Evelyn **(1903–1966)** *English journalist and novelist*

I expect you'll be becoming a schoolmaster, sir. That's what most of the gentlemen does, sir, that gets sent down for indecent behaviour.

Decline and Fall (1928) 'Prelude'

Anyone who has been to an English public school will always feel comparatively at home in prison. **Decline and Fall (1928)**

Wilde, Oscar **(1854–1900)** *Irish dramatist, novelist, critic and wit*

Complaining at having to wait in the rain for transport to take him to prison

If this is the way Queen Victoria treats her prisoners, she doesn't deserve to have any. **Attr.**

PUNISHMENT

Hubbard, Elbert **(1856–1915)** *American author and editor*

Men are not punished for their sins, but by them.

A Thousand and One Epigrams (1911)

Pepys, Samuel **(1633–1703)** *English diarist and civil servant*

I went out to Charing Cross, to see Major-General Harrison hanged, drawn and quartered; which was done there, he looking as cheerful as any man could do in that condition. **Diary, 1660**

Salmon, George **(1819–1904)** *Provost of Trinity College, Dublin*

On hearing a colleague claiming to have been caned only once in his life, and that, for telling the truth

Well, it certainly cured you, Mahaffy. **Attr.**

Vidal, Gore **(1925–)** *American novelist, dramatist, essayist, critic and poet*

When asked for his views about corporal punishment

I'm all for bringing back the birch, but only between consenting adults.

TV interview with David Frost

RACISM

Davis, Sammy, Junior **(1925–1990)** *American entertainer and singer*

Being a star has made it possible for me to get insulted in places where the average Negro could never hope to get insulted. **Yes I can (1965)**

De Blank, Joost **(1908–1968)** *Dutch-born clergyman and writer*

I suffer from an incurable disease – colour blindness. **Attr.**

Einstein, Albert **(1879–1955)** *German-Swiss American physicist*

If my theory of relativity is proven successful, Germany will claim me as a German and France will declare that I am a citizen of the world. Should my theory prove untrue, France will say that I am a German and Germany will declare that I am a Jew. **Address, c. 1929**

Forster, E.M. **(1879–1970)** *English novelist and critic*

The so-called white races are really pinko-gray.

A Passage to India (1924)

Marx, Groucho **(1895–1977)** *American film comedian*

When excluded, on racial grounds, from a beach club

Since my daughter is only half-Jewish, could she go into the water up to her knees? **The Observer, 1977**

Tutu, Archbishop Desmond **(1931–)** *South African prelate*

It is very difficult now to find anyone in South Africa who ever supported apartheid. **The Observer, 1994**

RELIGION

Barrie, Sir J.M. **(1860–1937)** *Scottish novelist and dramatist*

One's religion is whatever he is most interested in, and yours is Success. **The Twelve-Pound Look**

Behan, Brendan **(1923–1964)** *Irish author*

Pound notes are the best religion in the world.

The Wit of Brendan Behan (1968)

Butler, Samuel **(1835–1902)** *English novelist, painter and philosopher*

To be at all is to be religious more or less.

The Note-Books of Samuel Butler (1912)

Diderot, Denis **(1713–1784)** *French writer*

Wandering in a vast forest at night, I have only a faint light to guide me. A stranger appears and says to me: 'My friend, you should blow out your candle in order to find your way more clearly.' This stranger is a theologian. **Addition aux Pensées Philosophiques**

Ellis, Havelock **(1859–1939)** *English physician*

The whole religious complexion of the modern world is due to the absence from Jerusalem of a lunatic asylum.

Impressions and Comments (1914)

Fleming, Marjory **(1803–1811)** *Scottish child author*

I hope I will be religious again but as for regaining my character I despair for it. **In Esdaile (ed.), Journals, Letters and Verses (1934)**

Inge, William Ralph **(1860–1954)** *English prelate and mathematician*

To become a popular religion, it is only necessary for a superstition to enslave a philosophy. **Outspoken Essays**

Melbourne, Lord (1779–1848) *English Whig politician*

On listening to an evangelical sermon
Things have come to a pretty pass when religion is allowed to invade the sphere of private life.

In G.W.E. Russell, Collections and Recollections (1898)

Mencken, H.L. (1880–1956) *American journalist and linguist*

We must respect the other fellow's religion, but only in the sense and to the extent that we respect his theory that his wife is beautiful and his children smart. **Notebooks (1956)**

O'Casey, Sean (1880–1964) *Irish playwright*

There's no reason to bring religion into it. I think we ought to have as great a regard for religion as we can, so as to keep it out of as many things as possible. **The Plough and the Stars (1926)**

ROYALTY

Beerbohm, Sir Max (1872–1956) *English writer and caricaturist*

Have you ever noticed ... that all hot-water bottles look like Henry the Eighth? **In S.N. Behrman, Conversations with Max (1960)**

Disraeli, Benjamin (1804–1881) *English statesman and novelist*

In answer to Gladstone's taunt that Disraeli could make a joke of any subject, including Queen Victoria
Her Majesty is not a subject. **Attr.**

Farouk I (1920–1965) *Last King of Egypt, 1936–52*

Remark made to Lord Boyd-Orr, 1948
There will soon be only five kings left – the Kings of England, Diamonds, Hearts, Spades and Clubs. **Attr.**

George VI (1895–1952)

We're not a family; we're a firm. **Attr. in Lane, Our Future King**

Landor, Walter Savage (1775–1864) *English poet and prose writer*

George the First was always reckoned
Vile, but viler George the Second;
And what mortal ever heard
Any good of George the Third?
When from earth the Fourth descended
God be praised, the Georges ended! **The Atlas, 1855, 'Epigram'**

Sellar, Walter (1898–1951) and **Yeatman, Robert** (1897–1968)
British humorous writers

Charles II was always very merry and was therefore not so much a king as a Monarch. **1066 And All That (1930)**

Worsthorne, Sir Peregrine (1923–) *English writer and journalist*

A little more willingness to bore, and much less eagerness to entertain, would do the monarchy no end of good. **The Sunday Telegraph, 1993**

SCIENCE

Bridie, James **(1888–1951)** *Scottish dramatist*

Eve and the apple was the first great step in experimental science.

Mr Bolfry (1943)

Clarke, Arthur C. **(1917–)** *English science fiction writer*

Technology, sufficiently advanced, is indistinguishable from magic.

The Times, 1996

Cronenberg, David **(1943–)** *Canadian film director*

A virus is only doing its job. **The Sunday Telegraph, 1992**

Dagg, Fred **(1948–)** *New Zealand comic*

I can see ... why a man who lives in Colorado is so anxious for all this nuclear activity to go on in Australia, an area famed among nuclear scientists for its lack of immediate proximity to their own residential areas. **Dagshead Revisited (1989)**

Einstein, Albert **(1879–1955)** *German-Swiss American physicist*

When a man sits with a pretty girl for an hour, it seems like a minute. But let him sit on a hot stove for a minute – and it's longer than any hour. That's relativity. **Attr.**

Hay, Will **(1888–1949)** *British comedian*

Master: They split the atom by firing particles at it, at 5,500 miles a second.
Boy: Good heavens. And they only split it?

The Fourth Form at St Michael's (c. 1925), 'The Inkstains Theory'

Huxley, T.H. **(1825–1895)** *English biologist*

The great tragedy of Science – the slaying of a beautiful hypothesis by an ugly fact. **British Association Annual Report (1870)**

Philip, Prince, Duke of Edinburgh **(1921–)**
British consort of Queen Elizabeth II

Dentopedology is the science of opening your mouth and putting your foot in it. I've been practising it for years. **Attr.**

Pirsig, Robert **(1928–)** *American writer*

Traditional scientific method had always been at the very best, 20-20 hindsight. It's good for seeing where you've been.

Zen and the Art of Motorcycle Maintenance (1974)

Stenhouse, David **(1932–)** *New Zealand zoologist*

On the conservation of biological resources

I know a man who has a device for converting solar energy into food. Delicious stuff he makes with it, too. Being doing it for years ... It's called a farm. **Crisis in Abundance (1966)**

Thurber, James **(1894–1961)** *American humorist, writer and illustrator*

Her own mother lived the latter years of her life in the horrible suspicion that electricity was dripping invisibly all over the house.

My Life and Hard Times (1933)

Wilberforce, Bishop Samuel **(1805–1873)** *English prelate*

To T.H. Huxley

And, in conclusion, I would like to ask the gentleman ... whether the ape from which he is descended was on his grandmother's or his grandfather's side of the family. **Speech at Oxford, 1860**

THE SCOTS

Barrie, Sir J.M. **(1860–1937)** *Scottish novelist and dramatist*

There are few more impressive sights in the world than a Scotsman on the make. **What Every Woman Knows (1908)**

Boorde, Andrew **(c. 1490–1549)** *English Carthusian monk and physician*

Trust your no Skott. **Letter to Thomas Cromwell, 1536**

The devellysche dysposicion of a Scottysh man, not to love nor favour an Englishe man. **Letter to Thomas Cromwell, 1536**

Cleveland, John **(1613–1658)** *English Cavalier poet*

Had Cain been Scot, God would have changed his doom,
Nor forced him wander, but confined him home. **'The Rebel Scot' (1647)**

Ewart, Gavin **(1916–1995)** *English poet*

The Irish are great talkers
Persuasive and disarming,
You can say lots and lots
Against the Scots –
But at least they're never charming! **The Complete Little Ones (1986)**

Johnson, Samuel **(1709–1784)** *English lexicographer, poet and critic*

Much may be made of a Scotchman, if he be caught young.

In Boswell, The Life of Samuel Johnson (1791)

Keillor, Garrison **(1942–)** *American writer*

Lutherans are like Scottish people, only with less frivolity.

The Independent, 1992

North, Christopher **(1785–1854)** *Scottish critic and essayist*

Minds like ours, my dear James, must always be above national prejudices, and in all companies it gives me true pleasure to declare, that, as a people, the English are very little indeed inferior to the Scotch. **Blackwood's Edinburgh Magazine, 1826**

Scott, Alexander **(1920–1989)** *Scottish poet*

Damn
Aa. **Scotched, 'Scotch Religion'**

I tellt ye
I tellt ye. **Scotched, 'Scotch Education'**

Tidy, Bill *Cartoonist*

Glencoe is the only place in Scotland where they can't open a MacDonald's.

Wodehouse, P.G. **(1881–1975)** *English novelist*

It is never difficult to distinguish between a Scotsman with a grievance and a ray of sunshine.

Blandings Castle and Elsewhere (1935), 'The Custody of the Pumpkin'

THE SEASONS

Coleridge, Samuel Taylor **(1772–1834)** *English poet*

Summer has set in with its usual severity. **Letters of Charles Lamb (1888)**

Searle, Ronald **(1920–)** *English cartoonist*

In the spring ... your lovely Chloë lightly turns to one mass of spots.

The Terror of St Trinian's (1952)

Thurber, James **(1894–1961)** *American humorist, writer and illustrator*

I said the hounds of spring are on winter's traces – but let it pass, let it pass! **Cartoon caption**

SELF

Connolly, Cyril **(1903–1974)** *English author and journalist*

I have always disliked myself at any given moment; the total of such moments is my life. **Enemies of Promise (1938)**

Jacobi, Karl **(1804–1851)** *German mathematician*

On being mistaken by a lady for his brother
Pardon me, madam, but I am my brother.

In M.H. Jacobs, Men of Mathematics

Powell, Anthony **(1905–)** *English novelist*

He fell in love with himself at first sight and it is a passion to which he has always remained faithful. Self-love seems so often unrequited.

The Acceptance World (1955)

Twain, Mark **(1835–1910)** *American humorist and novelist*

When people do not respect us we are sharply offended; yet deep down in his heart no man much respects himself. **Notebooks (1935)**

Wilde, Oscar **(1854–1900)** *Irish dramatist, novelist, critic and wit*

Other people are quite dreadful. The only possible society is oneself.

An Ideal Husband (1895)

SEPARATION

Anonymous

When you've got over the disgrace of the single life, it's more airy.

Irish woman, quoted in broadcasts by Joyce Grenfell

Cope, Wendy **(1945–)** *English writer and poet*

The day he moved out was terrible –
That evening she went through hell.
His absence wasn't a problem
But the corkscrew had gone as well.

'Loss' (1992)

SEX

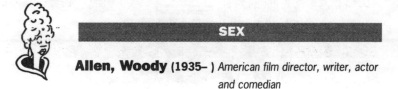

Allen, Woody **(1935–)** *American film director, writer, actor and comedian*

Is sex dirty? Only if it's done right.

Everything You Always Wanted to Know About Sex, film, 1972

Hey, don't knock masturbation! It's sex with someone I love.

Annie Hall, film, 1977

Referring to sex

It was the most fun I ever had without laughing.

Annie Hall, film, 1977

On bisexuality

It immediately doubles your chances for a date on Saturday night.

New York Times, 1975

I want to tell you a terrific story about oral contraception. I asked this girl to sleep with me and she said 'no'.

Attr.

Bankhead, Tallulah **(1903–1968)** *American actress*

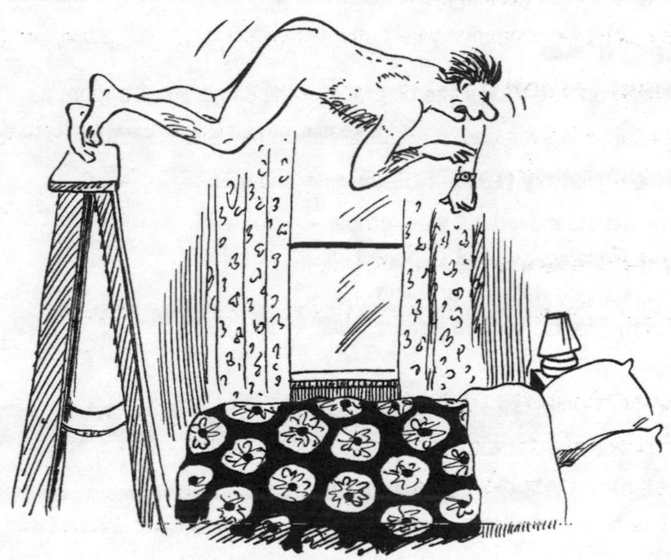

To an admirer

I'll come and make love to you at five o'clock. If I'm late start without me. **In E. Morgan, Somerset Maugham (1980)**

Benchley, Robert **(1889–1945)** *American humorist and actor*

Comment on an office shared with Dorothy Parker

One cubic foot less of space and it would have constituted adultery.

Attr.

Bradbury, Malcolm **(1932–)** *English novelist, critic and academic*

If God had meant us to have group sex, I guess he'd have given us all more organs. **Who Do You Think You Are? Stories and Parodies (1976)**

Byron, Lord **(1788–1824)** *English poet*

What men call gallantry, and gods adultery,
Is much more common where the climate's sultry. **Don Juan (1824)**

Heller, Joseph **(1923–)** *American novelist*

Prostitution gives her an opportunity to meet people. It provides fresh air and wholesome exercise, and it keeps her out of trouble.

Catch-22 (1961)

Huxley, Aldous **(1894–1963)** *English novelist*

Lady Capricorn, he understood, was still keeping open bed.

Antic Hay (1923)

Marx, Groucho **(1895–1977)** *American film comedian*

I want to register a complaint. Do you know who sneaked into my room at three o'clock this morning? – Who?
Nobody, and that's my complaint. **Monkey Business, film, 1931**

Whoever named it necking was a poor judge of anatomy. **Attr.**

Many years ago I chased a woman for almost two years, only to discover her tastes were exactly like mine: we were both crazy about girls. **Attr.**

Miller, Henry **(1891–1980)** *American novelist and essayist*

Sex is one of the nine reasons for reincarnation ... The other eight are unimportant. **Big Sur and the Oranges of Hieronymus Bosch**

Milligan, Spike **(1918–)** *English humorist*

Contraceptives should be used on every conceivable occasion.

The Last Goon Show of All

Nash, Ogden **(1902–1971)** *American humorous poet*

Home is heaven and orgies are vile
But you need an orgy, once in a while.

The Primrose Path (1935), 'Home, Sweet Home'

Parker, Dorothy **(1893–1967)** *American poet, writer, critic and wit*

Of the Yale Prom

If all the girls attending it were laid end to end, I wouldn't be at all surprised. **In Alexander Woollcott, While Rome Burns (1934)**

Remark when someone said, 'They're ducking for apples' at a Hallowe'en party

There, but for a typographical error, is the story of my life.

In J. Keats, You Might As Well Live (1970)

Sayers, Dorothy L. **(1893–1957)** *English novelist, dramatist and essayist*

As I grow older and older,
And totter towards the tomb,
I find that I care less and less
Who goes to bed with whom.

In Hitchman, Such a Strange Lady (1975)

Sharpe, Tom **(1928–)** *English comic novelist*

Skullion had little use for contraceptives at the best of times. Unnatural, he called them, and placed them in the lower social category of things along with elastic-sided boots and made-up bow ties. Not the sort of attire for a gentleman. **Porterhouse Blue (1974)**

Smith, Sydney **(1771–1845)** *English clergyman, essayist and wit*

As the French say, there are three sexes – men, women, and clergymen. **In Holland, A Memoir of the Reverend Sydney Smith (1855)**

Thurber, James **(1894–1961)** *American humorist, writer and illustrator*

On being accosted at a party by a drunk woman who claimed she would like to have a baby by him

Surely you don't mean by unartificial insemination! **Attr.**

Vidal, Gore **(1925–)** *American novelist, dramatist, essayist, critic and poet*

On being asked if his first sexual experience had been heterosexual or homosexual

I was too polite to ask. **Forum, 1987, 'First Sex'**

Waugh, Evelyn **(1903–1966)** *English journalist and novelist*

All this fuss about sleeping together. For physical pleasure I'd sooner go to my dentist any day. **Vile Bodies (1930)**

Wax, Ruby *American actress and television chat-show host*

This 'relationship' business is one big waste of time. It is just Mother Nature urging you to breed, breed, breed. Learn from nature. Learn from our friend the spider. Just mate once and then kill him.

Spectator, 1994

West, Mae **(1892–1980)** *American actress and scriptwriter*

Is that a gun in your pocket or are you just pleased to see me?

In J. Weintraub, Peel Me a Grape (1975)

SHOWBUSINESS

Anonymous

Can't act, can't sing, slightly bald. Can dance a little.

Comment by a Hollywood executive on Fred Astaire's first screen test

Bankhead, Tallulah (1903–1968) *American actress*

Said on dropping fifty dollars into a tambourine held out by a Salvation Army collector
Don't bother to thank me. I know what a perfectly ghastly season it's been for you Spanish dancers. **Attr.**

Davis, Bette (1908–1989) *American film actress*

Of a starlet
I see – she's the original good time that was had by all.

In Halliwell, Filmgoer's Book of Quotes (1973)

Goldwyn, Samuel (1882–1974) *Polish-born American film producer*

Directors [are] always biting the hand that lays the golden egg.

In Zierold, Moguls (1969)

Before the opening of his film The Best Years of Our Lives *in 1946*
I don't care if it doesn't make a nickel, I just want every man, woman, and child in America to see it. **In Zierold, Moguls (1969)**

To Jack L. Warner, when Goldwyn discovered that one of his directors was moonlighting for Warner Bros.; one of the few genuine Goldwynisms
How can we sit together and deal with this industry if you're going to do things like that to me? If this is the way you do it, gentlemen, include me out! **Quoted by S. Goldwyn Jnr, TV Times, 1982**

The trouble with this business is the dearth of bad pictures.

Attr., but probably apocryphal

What we want is a story that starts with an earthquake and works its way up to a climax. **Attr.**

I'M SORRY, SIR BUT YOU'RE SECOND SITTING, LAST SUPPER!

Querying the number of disciples appearing in his film The Last Supper
'Why only twelve?' 'That's the original number.' 'Well, go out and get thousands.' **Attr.**

Grable, Betty **(1916–1973)** *US film star and wartime 'pin-up'*

There are two reasons why I'm in show business, and I'm standing on both of them. **Attr.**

Grade, Lew **(1906–1994)** *British television producer*

All my shows are great. Some of them are bad. But they are all great. **The Observer, 1975**

Guinan, Texas **(1884–1933)** *Canadian actress*

When she and her troupe were refused entry to France in 1931
It goes to show that fifty million Frenchmen *can* be wrong. **Attr.**

Kaufman, George S. (1889–1961) *American journalist and scriptwriter*

At a rehearsal of the Marx Brothers film Animal Crackers *(1930), for which he wrote the script*

Excuse me for interrupting but I actually thought I heard a line I wrote.

In S. Meredith, George S. Kaufman and the Algonquin Round Table (1974)

Levant, Oscar (1906–1972) *American pianist*

Romance on the High Seas was Doris Day's first picture; that was before she became a virgin. **Memoirs of an Amnesiac (1965)**

Strip the phony tinsel off Hollywood and you'll find the real tinsel underneath. **In Halliwell, Filmgoer's Book of Quotes (1973)**

Marx, Chico (1886–1961) *US film comedian, eldest of the Marx Brothers*

Explanation given when his wife caught him kissing a chorus girl

But I wasn't kissing her. I was whispering in her mouth.

In G. Marx and R. Anobile, The Marx Brothers Scrapbook (1974)

Marx, Groucho (1895–1977) *American film comedian*

We in this industry know that behind every successful screenwriter stands a woman. And behind her stands his wife. **Attr.**

Explaining why he didn't go to films starring Victor Mature

I never go to movies where the hero's bust is bigger than the heroine's.

Attr.

Reed, Rex (1938–) *American film and music critic and columnist*

Cannes is where you lie on the beach and stare at the stars – or vice versa. **Attr.**

Rogers, Will (1879–1935) *American comic actor, rancher, writer and wit*

The movies are the only business where you can go out front and applaud yourself. **In Halliwell, Filmgoer's Book of Quotes (1973)**

Rowland, Richard **(c. 1881–1947)**

When United Artists was established in 1919 by Mary Pickford, Douglas Fairbanks, Charlie Chaplin and D.W. Griffith

The lunatics have taken over the asylum. **Attr.**

Sayle, Alexei **(1952–)** *English comedian, producer and columnist*

On compèring

I remember once telling Robin Williams he could only do 10 minutes. He offered to buy the club. **The Independent, 1992**

Skelton, Red **(1913–)** *American radio, television and film comedian*

Commenting on the large crowds attending the funeral of Hollywood producer Harry Cohn

It proves what they say, give the public what they want to see and they'll come out for it.

Remark, 1958; also attrib. to Samuel Goldwyn at Louis B. Mayer's funeral in 1957

Southern, Terry (1924–) *American novelist and screenwriter*

She says, 'Listen, who do I have to fuck to get off this picture?'

Blue Movie (1970)

Thomas, Irene (1920–) *English writer and broadcaster*

It was the kind of show where the girls are not auditioned – just measured. **Attr.**

Tracy, Spencer (1900–1967) *American film actor*

Explaining what he looked for in a script

Days off. **Attr.**

Defending his demand for equal billing with Katherine Hepburn

This is a movie, not a lifeboat. **Attr.**

Tree, Sir Herbert Beerbohm (1853–1917) *English actor-manager*

Directing a group of sophisticated actresses

Ladies, just a little more virginity, if you don't mind.

In H. Teichmann, Smart Aleck

West, Mae (1892–1980) *American actress and scriptwriter*

After her performance in Catherine the Great

I'm glad you like my Catherine. I like her too. She ruled thirty million people and had three thousand lovers. I do the best I can in two hours.

Speech from the stage

SIN

Anonymous

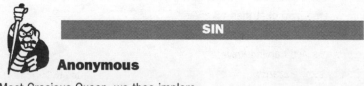

Most Gracious Queen, we thee implore
To go away and sin no more,
But if that effort be too great,
To go away at any rate.

Epigram on Queen Caroline, quoted in Lord Colchester's Diary, 1820

Coolidge, Calvin **(1872–1933)** *US President 1923–1929*

On being asked what had been said by a clergyman who preached on sin

He said he was against it. **Attr.**

West, Mae **(1892–1980)** *American actress and scriptwriter*

Whenever I'm caught between two evils, I take the one I've never tried.

Klondike Annie, film, 1936

Young, William Blamire **(1862–1935)** *Australian painter*

A mad little maid is Rose Madder,
As bad as they make 'em and badder.
At her window one night
Was the scandalous sight
Of a lad and, God help us, a ladder. **In R.H. Croll, I Recall ...**

SMOKING

Calverley, C.S. **(1831–1884)** *English poet*

How they who use fusees
All grow by slow degrees
Brainless as chimpanzees,
Meagre as lizards:
Go mad, and beat their wives;
Plunge (after shocking lives)
Razors and carving knives
Into their gizzards. **'Ode to Tobacco' (1861)**

Doyle, Sir Arthur Conan **(1859–1930)** *Scottish writer*

A little monograph on the ashes of one hundred and forty different varieties of pipe, cigar, and cigarette tobacco.

'The Boscombe Valley Mystery' (1892)

Kipling, Rudyard (1865–1936) *English writer*

PLACE THE CIGAR BETWEEN
THE THUMB AND FOREFINGERS
OF HIS RIGHT HAND..

And a woman is only a woman, but a good cigar is a Smoke.

'The Betrothed' (1886)

Lamb, Charles (1775–1834) *English essayist*

Dr Parr ... asked him, how he had acquired his power of smoking at such a rate? Lamb replied, 'I toiled after it, sir, as some men toil after virtue.' **In Talfourd, Memoirs of Charles Lamb (1892)**

Napoleon III (1808–1873) *French emperor*

On being asked to ban smoking

This vice brings in one hundred million francs in taxes every year. I will certainly forbid it at once – as soon as you can name a virtue that brings in as much revenue. **In Hoffmeister, Anekdotenschatz**

Twain, Mark **(1835–1910)** *American humorist and novelist*

Saying how easy it is to give up smoking
I've done it a hundred times! **Attr.**

Wilde, Oscar **(1854–1900)** *Irish dramatist, novelist, critic and wit*

A cigarette is the perfect type of a perfect pleasure. It is exquisite, and it leaves one unsatisfied. What more can one want?

The Picture of Dorian Gray (1891)

SOCIETY

Counihan, Noel Jack **(1913–1986)** *Australian artist*

In human society the warmth is mainly at the bottom. **Age, 1986**

Marx, Groucho **(1895–1977)** *American film comedian*

Please accept my resignation. I don't want to belong to any club that would have me as a member. **Groucho and Me (1959)**

Roosevelt, Theodore **(1858–1919)** *US President 1901–1912*

The men with the muck-rakes are often indispensable to the well-being of society; but only if they know when to stop raking the muck.

Speech, 1906

Smith, F.E. **(1872–1930)** *English lawyer and statesman*

We have the highest authority for believing that the meek shall inherit the Earth; though I have never found any particular corroboration of this aphorism in the records of Somerset House.

Contemporary Personalities (1924), 'Marquess Curzon'

Wilde, Oscar **(1854–1900)** *Irish dramatist, novelist, critic and wit*

Of society
To be in it is merely a bore. But to be out of it is simply a tragedy.

A Woman of No Importance (1893)

SPACE

Alfonso X **(1221–1284)** *King of Castile and Léon*

On the Ptolemaic system of astronomy
If the Lord Almighty had consulted me before embarking upon Creation, I should have recommended something simpler. **Attr.**

Chesterton, G.K. **(1874–1936)** *English novelist, poet and critic*

The cosmos is about the smallest hole that a man can hide his head in.
Orthodoxy (1908)

De Vries, Peter **(1910–1993)** *American novelist and humorist*

Anyone informed that the universe is expanding and contracting in pulsations of eighty billion years has a right to ask, 'What's in it for me?'
The Glory of the Hummingbird (1974)

Vidal, Gore **(1925–)** *American novelist, dramatist, essayist, critic and poet*

The astronauts! ... Rotarians in outer space. **Two Sisters (1970)**

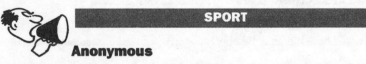

SPORT

Anonymous

Shooting is a popular sport in the countryside ... Unlike many other countries, the outstanding characteristic of the sport has been that it is not confined to any one class.
The Northern Ireland Tourist Board, 1969

They'll be dancing in the streets of Raith tonight.
Falsely attributed to both Kenneth Wolstenholme and David Coleman, this reference to Raith Rovers fans dancing in a non-existent Scottish town – the team plays in Kirkcaldy – almost certainly originated in a BBC radio broadcast from London in 1963, after Raith Rovers defeated Aberdeen in a Scottish Cup tie

'Well, what sort of sport has Lord — had?'
'Oh, the young Sahib shot divinely, but God was very merciful to the birds.' **In Russell, Collections and Recollections (1898)**

Barbarito, Luigi (1922–) *Italian archbishop and diplomat*

Papal emissary, commenting on a sponsored snooker competition at a convent

Playing snooker gives you firm hands and helps to build up character. It is the ideal recreation for dedicated nuns. **The Daily Telegraph, 1989**

Bennett, Alan (1934–) *English dramatist, actor and diarist*

If you think squash is a competitive activity, try flower arrangement.

Talking Heads (1988)

Bernhardt, Sarah (1844–1923) *French actress*

Remark while watching a game of football
I do love cricket – it's so very English. **Attr.**

Canterbury, Tom *American basketball player*

The trouble with referees is that they just don't care which side wins.
The Guardian, 1980

Coleman, David (1926–) *English sports commentator*

That's the fastest time ever run – but it's not as fast as the world record. **In Fantoni, Private Eye's Colemanballs (3) (1986)**

Connolly, Billy (1942–) *Scottish comedian*

The three saddest words in the English language: Partick Thistle nil.
Attr.

Crooks, Garth (1958–) *English footballer*

Football is football; if that weren't the case, it wouldn't be the game it is. **In Fantoni, Private Eye's Colemanballs (2) (1984)**

Duffy, Jim *Scottish football manager*

Of goalkeeper Andy Murdoch
He has an answerphone installed on his six-yard line and the message says: 'Sorry, I'm not in just now, but if you'd like to leave the ball in the back of the net, I'll get back to you as soon as I can.'

In Umbro Book of Football Quotations (1993)

Ford, Henry (1863–1947) *American automobile manufacturer*

Exercise is bunk. If you are healthy, you don't need it: if you are sick, you shouldn't take it. **Attr.**

Johnson, Samuel (1709–1784) *English lexicographer, poet and critic*

It is very strange, and very melancholy, that the paucity of human pleasures should persuade us ever to call hunting one of them.

In Piozzi, Anecdotes of the Late Samuel Johnson (1786)

Fly fishing may be a very pleasant amusement; but angling or float fishing I can only compare to a stick and a string, with a worm at one end and a fool at the other.

Attr. in Hawker, Instructions to Young Sportsmen (1859)

Mourie, Graham (1952–) *New Zealand rugby player*

Nobody ever beats Wales at rugby, they just score more points.

In Keating, Caught by Keating

O'Reilly, Tony (1936–) *Irish rugby player*

Commenting on the voice of Winston McCarthy, the noted rugby commentator
The love call of two pieces of sandpaper. **New Zealand Listener, 1984**

O'Rourke, P.J. (1947–) *American writer and humorist*

The sport of skiing consists of wearing three thousand dollars' worth of clothes and equipment and driving two hundred miles in the snow in order to stand around at a bar and get drunk. **Modern Manners (1984)**

Palmer, Arnold (1929–) *American golfer*

Replying to an onlooker who observed that he was playing so well he must have plenty of luck on his side
The more I practise the luckier I get. **Attr.**

Shankly, Bill (1914–1981) *Scottish footballer and manager*

Some people think football is a matter of life and death. I don't like that attitude. I can assure them it is much more serious than that.

Remark on BBC TV, 1981

Shaw, George Bernard (1856–1950) *Irish dramatist and critic*

An R.S.V.P. to an invitation to attend an athletic meeting at the Wangamui Domain

I take athletic competitive sports very seriously indeed ... as they seem to produce more bad feeling, bad manners and international hatred than any other popular movement. **Auckland Star, 1934**

Snagge, John (1904–1996) *British broadcaster*

I don't know who's ahead – it's either Oxford or Cambridge.

Radio commentary on the Boat Race, 1949

Stubbes, Philip (c. 1555–1610) *English Puritan pamphleteer*

Football ... causeth fighting, brawling, contention, quarrel picking, murder, homicide and great effusion of blood, as daily experience teacheth. **Anatomy of Abuses (1583)**

Viera, Ondina *Uruguayan football manager*

Other nations have history. We have football. **The Spectator, 1996**

Wilde, Oscar (1854–1900) *Irish dramatist, novelist, critic and wit*

The English country gentleman galloping after a fox – the unspeakable in full pursuit of the uneatable. **A Woman of No Importance (1893)**

Wodehouse, P.G. (1881–1975) *English novelist*

The least thing upset him on the links. He missed short putts because of the uproar of the butterflies in the adjoining meadows.

The Clicking of Cuthbert (1922)

TAX

Burke, Edmund (1729–1797) *Irish statesman and philosopher*

To tax and to please, no more than to love and to be wise, is not given to men. **Speech on American Taxation (1774)**

Capone, Al (1899–1947) *American gangster*

Objecting to the US Bureau of Internal Revenue claiming large sums in unpaid back tax

They can't collect legal taxes from illegal money. **In Kobler, Capone (1971)**

Rogers, Will (1879–1935) *American comic actor, rancher, writer and wit*

Income tax has made more liars out of American people than golf.

The Illiterate Digest (1924), 'Helping the Girls with their Income Taxes'

Shaw, George Bernard (1856–1950) *Irish dramatist and critic*

A government which robs Peter to pay Paul can always depend on the support of Paul. **Everybody's Political What's What (1944)**

Smith, Adam (1723–1790) *Scottish economist and philosopher*

There is no art which one government sooner learns of another than that of draining money from the pockets of the people.

Wealth of Nations (1776)

TELEVISION

Anonymous

This must be the first time a rat has come to the aid of a sinking ship.

BBC spokesman on the success of puppet Roland Rat at TV-am, 1983

Coren, Alan (1938–) *British humorist, writer and broadcaster*

Television is more interesting than people. If it were not, we should have people standing in the corners of our rooms. **Attr.**

Coward, Sir Noël (1899–1973) *English dramatist, actor and composer*

Television is for appearing on, not looking at. **Attr.**

Debray, Régis (1942–) *French Marxist theorist*

The darkest spot in modern society is a small luminous screen.

Teachers, Writers, Celebrities

Frost, David (1939–) *English broadcaster*

Television is an invention that permits you to be entertained in your living room by people you wouldn't have in your home. **Remark, 1971**

Hitchcock, Alfred (1899–1980) *English film director*

Television has brought murder back into the home – where it belongs.

The Observer, 1965

Scott, C.P. (1846–1932) *English newspaper editor*

Television? The word is half Latin and half Greek. No good can come of it. **Attr.**

Sheen, J. Fulton (1895–1979) *American Roman Catholic archbishop*

Referring to his contract for a television appearance

The big print giveth and the fine print taketh away. **Attr.**

TEMPTATION

Belloc, Hilaire (1870–1953) *French-born English writer and poet*

The Devil, having nothing else to do,
Went off to tempt My Lady Poltagrue.

My Lady, tempted by a private whim,
To his extreme annoyance, tempted him.

Sonnets and Verse (1923), 'On Lady Poltagrue: A Public Peril'

Graham, Clementina Stirling (1782–1877) *English writer*

The best way to get the better of temptation is just to yield to it.

Mystifications (1859)

Wilde, Oscar (1854–1900) *Irish dramatist, novelist, critic and wit*

I couldn't help it. I can resist everything except temptation.

Lady Windermere's Fan (1892)

THE THEATRE

Agate, James (1877–1947) *English dramatic critic and novelist*

Long experience has taught me that in England nobody goes to the theatre unless he or she has bronchitis. **Attr.**

Theatre director: a person engaged by the management to conceal the fact that the players cannot act. **Attr.**

Anonymous

How different, how very different from the home life of our own dear Queen! **Remark by woman at performance of Cleopatra by Sarah Bernhardt**

Bernard, Tristan (1866–1947) *French comic novelist and dramatist*

In the theatre the audience want to be surprised – but by things that they expect. **Attr.**

Cook, Peter (1937–1995) *English comic writer and comedian*

You know, I go to the theatre to be entertained ... I don't want to see plays about rape, sodomy and drug addiction ... I can get all that at home. **The Observer, caption to cartoon, 1962**

Gilbert, W.S. (1836–1911) *English librettist*

Speaking to an actor after he had given a poor performance
My dear chap! Good isn't the word! **Attr.**

Referring to Sir Henry Irving's Hamlet
Funny without being vulgar. **Attr.**

Gosse, Sir Edmund (1849–1928) *English poet and critic*

Referring to one of Swinburne's plays

We were as nearly bored as enthusiasm would permit.

In C. Hassall, Biography of Edward Marsh

Hopper, Hedda (1890–1966) *American actress and columnist*

At one time I thought he wanted to be an actor. He had certain qualifications, including no money and a total lack of responsibility.

From Under My Hat (1953)

Kaufman, George S. (1889–1961) *American journalist and scriptwriter*

On Raymond Massey's interpretation of Abraham Lincoln

Massey won't be satisfied until somebody assassinates him.

In S. Meredith, George S. Kaufman and the Algonquin Round Table (1974)

Kemble, John Philip (1757–1823) *English Shakespearian actor*

Said during a play which was continually interrupted by a crying child

Ladies and gentlemen, unless the play is stopped, the child cannot possibly go on. **Attr.**

Parker, Henry Taylor (1867–1934) *American journalist and critic*

Rebuking some talkative members of an audience, near whom he was sitting

Those people on the stage are making such a noise I can't hear a word you're saying. **In L. Humphrey, The Humor of Music**

Saki (Hector Hugh Munro) (1870–1916) *British journalist and writer*

Sherard Blaw, the dramatist who had discovered himself, and who had given so ungrudgingly of his discovery to the world.

The Unbearable Bassington (1912)

Shaw, George Bernard (1856–1950) *Irish dramatist and critic*

Responding to an offer by a producer to present one of Shaw's plays, having earlier rejected it

Better never than late. **In Oscar Levant, The Unimportance of Being Oscar**

Responding to a solitary boo amongst the mid-act applause at the first performance of Arms and the Man *in 1894*

I quite agree with you, sir, but what can two do against so many?

Oxford Book of Literary Anecdotes

Sheridan, Richard Brinsley (1751–1816) *Irish comic dramatist*

At a coffee house, during the fire which destroyed his Drury Lane theatre, 1809

A man may surely be allowed to take a glass of wine by his own fireside. **In Moore, Memoirs of the Life of Sheridan (1825)**

THOUGHT

Allen, Woody (1935–) *American film director, writer, actor and comedian*

My brain: it's my second favourite organ. **Sleeper, film, 1973**

Asquith, Margot (1864–1945) *Scottish political hostess and prose writer*

On F.E. Smith

He's very clever, but sometimes his brains go to his head.

Quoted by Baroness Asquith in TV programme, As I Remember, 1967

Bierce, Ambrose (1842–c. 1914) *American writer, journalist and soldier*

Brain: An apparatus with which we think that we think.

The Cynic's Word Book (1906)

James, William (1842–1910) *American philosopher and psychologist*

A great many people think they are thinking when they are merely rearranging their prejudices. **Attr**

Loos, Anita (1893–1981) *American humorous novelist and screenwriter*

So this gentleman said a girl with brains ought to do something with them besides think. **Gentlemen Prefer Blondes (1925)**

Mahaffy, Sir John Pentland (1839–1919) *Irish classical scholar*

My dear Oscar, you are not clever enough for us in Dublin. You had better run over to Oxford.

In H. Montgomery Hyde, Oscar Wilde: A Biography (1975)

Marquis, Don (1878–1937) *American columnist, satirist and poet*

An idea isn't responsible for the people who believe in it. **New York Sun**

Marx, Groucho (1895–1977) *American film comedian*

You've got the brain of a four-year-old boy, and I bet he was glad to get rid of it. **Horse Feathers, film, 1932**

Radcliffe-Brown, Alfred Reginald (1881–1955)
British social anthropologist, educator and author

On the anthropologist and reformer, Daisy Bates
The contents of her mind ... were somewhat similar to the contents of a well-stored sewing-basket after half a dozen kittens had been playing there undisturbed for a few days.

In E.L. Grant Watson, But to What Purpose

Stevenson, Adlai (1900–1965) *American lawyer and statesman*

Eggheads of the world unite; you have nothing to lose but your yolks.

Attr.

Valéry, Paul (1871–1945) *French poet and writer*

A gloss on Descartes
Sometimes I think: and sometimes I am.

The Faber Book of Aphorisms (1962)

TIME

Belloc, Hilaire (1870–1953) *French-born English writer and poet*

I am a sundial, and I make a botch
Of what is done far better by a watch.

Sonnets and Verse (second ed. 1938), 'On a Sundial'

Berlioz, Hector (1803–1869) *French composer*

Time is a great teacher, but unfortunately it kills all its pupils. **Attr.**

Emerson, Ralph Waldo (1803–1882) *American poet*

To a person complaining that he had not enough time
'Well,' said Red Jacket, 'I suppose you have all there is.'

'Works and Days' (1870)

Marx, Groucho (1895–1977) *American film comedian*

Time wounds all heels. **Attr.**

Rogers, Will (1879–1935) *American comic actor, rancher, writer and wit*

Half our life is spent trying to find something to do with the time we have rushed through life trying to save. **The New York Times, 1930**

Stoppard, Tom (1937–) *British stage, screen and radio dramatist*

Eternity's a terrible thought. I mean, where's it all going to end?

Rosencrantz and Guildenstern Are Dead (1967)I

Tree, Sir Herbert Beerbohm (1853–1917) *English actor-manager*

Remark to a man carrying a grandfather clock in the street

My poor fellow, why not carry a watch?

In Hesketh Pearson, Beerbohm Tree (1956)

TRAVEL

Benchley, Robert (1889–1945) *American humorist and actor*

Telegram sent on arriving in Venice

Streets flooded. Please advise. **Attr.**

Brien, Alan (1925–) *British novelist and journalist*

I have done almost every human activity inside a taxi which does not require main drainage. **Punch, 1972**

Buller, Arthur (1874–1944) *English botanist and mycologist*

There was a young lady named Bright,
Whose speed was far faster than light;
She set out one day
In a relative way,
And returned home the previous night. **Punch, 1923**

Bygraves, Max (1922–) *English singer, entertainer and TV personality*

Of Melbourne

I've always wanted to see a ghost town. You couldn't even get a parachute to open here after 10 p.m. **Melbourne Sun, 1965**

Cherry-Garrard, Apsley (1886–1959) *English polar explorer*

Polar exploration is at once the cleanest and most isolated way of having a bad time which has been devised.

The Worst Journey in the World (1922)

Chesterton, G.K. (1874–1936) *English novelist, poet and critic*

Telegram to his wife; other venues have been suggested but this was the original
Am in Market Harborough. Where ought I to be?

In M. Ward, Return to Chesterton (1952)

Coren, Alan (1938–) *British humorist, writer and broadcaster*

No visit to Dove Cottage, Grasmere, is complete without examining the outhouse where Hazlitt's father, a Unitarian minister of strong liberal views, attempted to put his hand up Dorothy Wordsworth's skirt.

All Except the Bastard (1969), 'Bohemia'

Of Switzerland
Since both its national products, snow and chocolate, melt, the cuckoo clock was invented solely in order to give tourists something solid to remember it by.

The Sanity Inspector (1974), 'All You Ever Need to Know about Europe'

Cowper, William (1731–1800) *English poet*

How much a dunce that has been sent to roam
Excels a dunce that has been kept at home. **'The Progress of Error' (1782)**

De Wolfe, Elsie (1865–1950) *American actress and interior designer*

On first sighting the Acropolis
It's beige! My color! **In J. Smith, Elsie de Wolfe**

Drew, Elizabeth (1887–1965)

Too often travel, instead of broadening the mind, merely lengthens the conversation. **The Literature of Gossip (1964)**

Flanders, Michael (1922–1975) *English lyricist* and **Swann, Donald** (1923–1994) *English composer and pianist*

If God had intended us to fly, he'd never have given us the railways.

'By Air', 1963

Galbraith J.K. (1908–) *Canadian-born American economist and author*

The Great Wall, I've been told, is the only man-made structure on earth that is visible from the moon. For the life of me I cannot see why anyone would go to the moon to look at it, when, with almost the same difficulty, it can be viewed in China. **The Sunday Times Magazine**

George VI **(1895–1952)**

Abroad is bloody. **In Auden, A Certain World (1970)**

Godley, A.D. **(1856–1925)** *English classical scholar, orator and satirist*

What is this that roareth thus?
Can it be a Motor Bus?
Yes, the smell and hideous hum
Indicate Motorem Bum! **'The Motor Bus', in a letter to C.R.L. Fletcher, 1914**

Graham, Harry **(1874–1936)** *British writer and journalist*

Aunt Jane observed, the second time
She tumbled off a bus,
'The step is short from the Sublime
To the Ridiculous.' **Ruthless Rhymes for Heartless Homes (1899), 'Equanimity'**

Johnson, Samuel **(1709–1784)** *English lexicographer, poet and critic*

Of the Giant's Causeway
Worth seeing? yes; but not worth going to see.

In Boswell, The Life of Samuel Johnson (1791)

O'Brien, Flann **(1911–1966)** *Irish novelist and journalist*

People who spend most of their natural lives riding iron bicycles over the rocky roadsteads of this parish get their personalities mixed up with the personalities of their bicycles as a result of the interchanging of the atoms of each of them and you would be surprised at the number of people in these parts who nearly are half people and half bicycles.

The Third Policeman (1967)

Robbins, Tom **(1936–)** *American novelist*

Human beings were invented by water as a device for transporting itself from one place to another. **Another Roadside Attraction (1971)**

Santayana, George **(1863–1952)** *Spanish philosopher and poet*

On being asked why he always travelled third class
Because there's no fourth class.

In Thomas, Living Biographies of the Great Philosophers

Thomson, Joseph (1858–1895) *Scottish explorer, geologist and writer*

His reply when J.M. Barrie asked what was the most hazardous part of his expedition to Africa

Crossing Piccadilly Circus. **In D. Dunbar, J.M. Barrie**

Vizinczey, Stephen (1933–) *Hungarian-born writer and broadcaster*

I was told I am a true cosmopolitan. I am unhappy everywhere.

The Guardian

White, E.B. (1899–1985) *American novelist, poet and parodist*

Commuter – one who spends his life
In riding to and from his wife;
A man who shaves and takes a train,
And then rides back to shave again. **'The Commuter' (1982)**

TRUTH

Agar, Herbert Sebastian (1897–1980) *American journalist and diplomat*

The truth which makes men free is for the most part the truth which men prefer not to hear. **A Time for Greatness (1942)**

Anonymous

Se non è vero, è molto ben trovato. [If it is not true, it is a happy invention.] **16th century**

Balfour, A.J. (1848–1930) *Scottish statesman and philosopher*

It is unfortunate, considering that enthusiasm moves the world, that so few enthusiasts can be trusted to speak the truth.

Letter to Mrs Drew, 1891

Bolingbroke, Henry (1678–1751)

Plain truth will influence half a score of men at most in a nation, or an age, while mystery will lead millions by the nose. **Letter, 1721**

Burns, George (1896–1996) *American comedian*

Sincerity. If you can fake that ... you've got it made.

Attr.; also attributed to Leo Rosten

Carroll, Lewis **(1832–1898)** *English mathematician and children's novelist*

What I tell you three times is true. **'The Hunting of the Snark' (1876)**

Cowper, William **(1731–1800)** *English poet*

And diff'ring judgments serve but to declare
That truth lies somewhere, if we knew but where. **'Hope' (1782)**

Darling, Charles **(1849–1936)** *English judge*

Much truth is spoken, that more may be concealed.

Scintillae Juris (1877)

Johnson, Samuel **(1709–1784)** *English lexicographer, poet and critic*

On sceptics

Truth, Sir, is a cow which will yield such people no more milk, and so they are gone to milk the bull. **In Boswell, The Life of Samuel Johnson (1791)**

La Bruyère, Jean de **(1645–1696)** *French writer*

Il y a quelques rencontres dans la vie où la vérité et la simplicité sont le meilleur manège du monde. [There are some circumstances in life where truth and simplicity are the best strategy in the world.]

Les caractères ou les moeurs de ce siècle (1688)

Leacock, Stephen **(1869–1944)** *Canadian humorist and economist*

A half truth in argument, like a half brick, carries better.

In Flesch, The Book of Unusual Quotations

Le Gallienne, Richard **(1866–1947)** *English writer*

Of Oscar Wilde

Paradox with him was only Truth standing on its head to attract attention. **The Romantic 90s**

Samuel, Lord **(1870–1963)** *English Liberal statesman and philosopher*

A truism is on that account none the less true.

A Book of Quotations (1947)

Solzhenitsyn, Alexander **(1918–)** *Russian writer*

When truth is discovered by someone else, it loses something of its attractiveness. **Candle in the Wind**

Twain, Mark **(1835–1910)** *American humorist and novelist*

When in doubt, tell the truth. **Pudd'nhead Wilson's New Calendar**

Wilde, Oscar **(1854–1900)** *Irish dramatist, novelist, critic and wit*

If one tells the truth, one is sure, sooner or later, to be found out.

The Chameleon, 1894, 'Phrases and Philosophies for the Use of the Young'

WAR

Austen, Jane **(1775–1817)** *English novelist*

Of the Battle of Albuera in 1811

How horrible it is to have so many people killed! – And what a blessing that one cares for none of them! **Letter to Cassandra Austen, 1811**

Bennett, Alan **(1934–)** *English dramatist, actor and diarist*

I have never understood this liking for war. It panders to instincts already catered for within the scope of any respectable domestic establishment. **Forty Years On (1969)**

Betjeman, Sir John **(1906–1984)** *English poet*

Gracious Lord, oh bomb the Germans.
Spare their women for Thy Sake,
And if that is not too easy
We will pardon Thy Mistake.
But, gracious Lord, whate'er shall be,
Don't let anyone bomb me.

Old Lights for New Chancels (1940), 'In Westminster Abbey'

Borges, Jorge Luis **(1899–1986)** *Argentinian writer*

On the Falklands War of 1982

The Falklands thing was a fight between two bald men over a comb.

Time, 1983

Carroll, Lewis **(1832–1898)** *English mathematician and children's novelist*

'You know,' he added very gravely, 'it's one of the most serious things that can possibly happen to one in a battle – to get one's head cut off.'

Through the Looking-Glass (1872)

Clemenceau, Georges **(1841–1929)** *French statesman*

La guerre! C'est une chose trop grave pour la confier à des militaires. [War is much too serious a thing to be left to the military.]

In Suarez, Sixty Years of French History: Clemenceau

Hirohito, Emperor **(1901–1989)**

The war situation has developed not necessarily to Japan's advantage.
Announcing Japan's surrender, 15 August 1945

Hope, Alec **(1907–)** *Australian poet and critic*

An ironic parody of the Greek epitaph commemorating the Spartans who died at Thermopylae in 480 BC
Go tell those old men, safe in bed,
We took their orders and are dead. **'Inscription for Any War'**

Lloyd George, David **(1863–1945)** *Welsh Liberal statesman*

Referring to the popular opinion that World War I would be the last major war
This war, like the next war, is a war to end war. **Attr.**

McLennan, Murdoch **(fl. 1715)** *Scottish poet*

There's some say that we wan, some say that they wan,
Some say that nane wan at a', man;
But one thing I'm sure, that at Sheriffmuir
A battle there was which I saw, man:
And we ran, and they ran, and they ran, and we ran,
And we ran; and they ran awa', man!
Roxburghe Ballads (1889), 'Sheriffmuir'

Michaelis, John H. **(1912–1985)** *US army officer*

Said to his regiment during the Korean War
You're not here to die for your country. You're here to make those – die for theirs. **Attr.**

Montague, C.E. **(1867–1928)** *English novelist*

War hath no fury like a non-combatant. **Disenchantment (1922)**

Pyrrhus **(319–272** BC**)** *King of Epirus*

After a hard-won battle
If we are victorious against the Romans in one more battle we shall be utterly ruined. **In Plutarch, Lives**

Rogers, Will **(1879–1935)** *American comic actor, rancher, writer and wit*

You can't say civilization don't advance, however, for in every war they kill you a new way. **The New York Times, 1929**

Sandburg, Carl (1878–1967) *American poet*

Sometime they'll give a war and nobody will come.

The People, Yes (1936)

Spooner, William (1844–1930) *English clergyman and university warden*

To an Oxford undergraduate after the First World War

Was it you or your brother who was killed in the war? **Attr.**

Strachey, Lytton (1880–1932) *English biographer and critic*

Reply when asked by a Tribunal what he, as a conscientious objector, would do if he saw a German soldier trying to rape his sister

I should try and come between them.

In Michael Holroyd, Lytton Strachey: A Critical Biography (1968)

Waugh, Evelyn (1903–1966) *English journalist and novelist*

When the war broke out she took down the signed photograph of the Kaiser and, with some solemnity, hung it in the menservants' lavatory; it was her one combative action. **Vile Bodies (1930)**

Giving his opinions of warfare after the battle of Crete, 1941

Like German opera, too long and too loud. **Attr.**

Williams, Robin (c.1951–) *American actor and comedian*

In a world without men, there would be no war – just intense negotiations every 28 days. **Robin Williams at the Met One-Man Show**

WEATHER

Gogarty, Oliver St John (1878–1957) *Irish poet, dramatist and writer*

In my best social accent I addressed him. I said, 'It is most extraordinary weather for this time of year!' He replied, 'Ah, it isn't this time of year at all.' **It Isn't This Time of Year at All (1954)**

Pound, Ezra (1885–1972) *American poet and critic*

Winter is icummen in,
Lhude sing Goddamn,
Raineth drop and staineth slop,
And how the wind doth ramm!
Sing: Goddamn. **'Ancient Music' (1916)**

Smith, Logan Pearsall (1865–1946) *American-born British writer*

Thank heavens, the sun has gone in, and I don't have to go out and enjoy it. **All Trivia (1933), 'Last Words'**

Smith, Sydney (1771–1845) *English clergyman, essayist and wit*

Discussing the recent hot weather

Heat, Ma'am! It was so dreadful here, that I found there was nothing left for it but to take off my flesh and sit in my bones.

In Holland, A Memoir of the Reverend Sydney Smith (1855)

WOMEN

Beerbohm, Sir Max (1872–1956) *English writer and caricaturist*

Most women are not so young as they are painted.

The Works of Max Beerbohm (1896), 'A Defence of Cosmetics'

Butler, Samuel (1835–1902) *English novelist, painter and philosopher*

Brigands demand your money or your life; women require both. **Attr.**

Ekland, Britt (1942–)

As a single woman with a child, I would love to have a wife.

The Independent (1994)

Johnson, Samuel (1709–1784) *English lexicographer, poet and critic*

Sir, a woman's preaching is like a dog's walking on his hinder legs. It is not done well; but you are surprised to find it done at all.

In Boswell, The Life of Samuel Johnson (1791)

Lerner, Alan Jay (1918–1986) *American lyricist and screenwriter*

There is no greater fan of the opposite sex than me, and I have the bills to prove it. **Attr.**

MacDonald, Sir John A. (1815–1891) *Canadian statesman*

Exchange between an irate suffragette and Sir John A. MacDonald when he was Prime Minister

Q. What is the difference between the Prime Minister and myself?

A. Madame, I cannot conceive. **Attr.**

Maugham, William Somerset **(1874–1965)** *British writer*

A woman will always sacrifice herself if you give her the opportunity. It is her favourite form of self-indulgence. **The Circle (1921)**

Mencken, H.L. **(1880–1956)** *American journalist and linguist*

When women kiss, it always reminds me of prize-fighters shaking hands. **Attr.**

Nash, Ogden **(1902–1971)** *American humorous poet*

Women would rather be right than reasonable.

Good Intentions (1942), 'Frailty, Thy Name is a Misnomer'

Rowland, Helen **(1875–1950)** *American writer*

It takes a woman twenty years to make a man of her son, and another woman twenty minutes to make a fool of him.

Reflections of a Bachelor Girl (1909)

Tucker, Sophie **(1884–1966)** *Russian-born American vaudeville singer*

From birth to eighteen, a girl needs good parents. From eighteen to thirty-five, she needs good looks. From thirty-five to fifty-five, she needs a good personality. From fifty-five on, she needs good cash.

In Michael Freedland, Sophie (1978)

Vanbrugh, Sir John **(1664–1726)** *English comic dramatist and architect*

Once a woman has given you her heart you can never get rid of the rest of her. **The Relapse, or Virtue in Danger (1696)**

Ward, Artemus **(1834–1867)** *American humorist; journalist, editor and lecturer*

The female woman is one of the greatest institooshuns of which this land can boste. **Artemus Ward, His Book (1862), 'Woman's Rights'**

West, Mae **(1892–1980)** *American actress and scriptwriter*

Referring to Delilah

I have a lot of respect for that dame. There's one lady barber that made good. **Goin' to Town, film, 1935**

Wodehouse, P.G. **(1881–1975)** *English novelist*

I can honestly say that I always look on Pauline as one of the nicest girls I was ever engaged to. **Thank You Jeeves (1934)**

WORK

Anonymous

In his chamber, weak and dying,
While the Norman Baron lay,
Loud, without, his men were crying,
'Shorter hours and better pay'. **'A Strike among the Poets'**

Benchley, Robert **(1889–1945)** *American humorist and actor*

I do most of my work sitting down; that's where I shine. **Attr.**

Clarke, John **(fl. 1639)**

He that would thrive
Must rise at five;
He that hath thriven
May lie till seven. **Paraemiologia Anglo-Latina (1639)**

Coward, Sir Noël **(1899–1973)** *English dramatist, actor and composer*

Work is much more fun than fun. **The Observer, 1963**

Jerome, Jerome K. **(1859–1927)** *English humorous writer*

I like work; it fascinates me. I can sit and look at it for hours. I love to keep it by me: the idea of getting rid of it nearly breaks my heart.

Three Men in a Boat (1889)

Parkinson, Cyril Northcote **(1909–1993)** *English political scientist*

Work expands so as to fill the time available for its completion.

Parkinson's Law (1958)

Peter, Laurence J. **(1919–1990)** *Canadian author, educator and psychologist*

In a hierarchy every employee tends to rise to his level of incompetence. **The Peter Principle – Why Things Always Go Wrong (1969)**

Philip, Prince, Duke of Edinburgh **(1921–)** *British consort of Queen Elizabeth II*

Replying to a query as to what nature of work he did

I am self-employed. **Attr.**

Reagan, Ronald (1911–) *Politician and film actor; US President 1981–89*

They say hard work never hurt anybody, but I figure why take the chance. **Attr.**

Spooner, William (1844–1930) *English clergyman and university warden*

You will find as you grow older that the weight of rages will press harder and harder upon the employer. **In William Hayter, Spooner (1977)**

Whitehorn, Katherine (1926–) *English journalist and writer*

The best careers advice to give to the young is 'Find out what you like doing best and get someone to pay you for doing it.' **The Observer, 1975**

Wilde, Oscar (1854–1900) *Irish dramatist, novelist, critic and wit*

Work is the curse of the drinking classes.

In H. Pearson, Life of Oscar Wilde (1946)

INDEX OF SOURCES

INDEX OF SOURCES